The Rooster Diaries
Nuggets of Wisdom, Whimsy, and Woe

Holly Coop

Copyright © 2025 Holly Coop

All rights reserved.

ISBN: 979-8-9911032-4-4

Cover Photo: Holly Coop
Cover Design: Mauverneen Blevins

DEDICATION

Family, friends, neighbors, and everyone in between.

Memories of you mean everything to me.

CONTENTS

Acknowledgements i

1	Beginnings	Pg 1
2	Spring	Pg 32
3	Planting Seeds	Pg 55
4	VIP's	Pg 82
5	Middle Ground	Pg 112
6	Summer	Pg 149
7	Pulling Weeds	Pg 167
8	Memories	Pg 210
9	Autumn	Pg 256
10	Endings	Pg 271
11	Winter	Pg 313

ACKNOWLEDGMENTS

Tom,
Thank you for being my fan.
Blessed to have called you, my friend.
I hope you knew, you were one of my favorite poets, too.
You inspired, motivated, and encouraged all who knew you.
You are missed.

The Rooster Diaries is a compilation of pieces originally published on my blog HollyCoopAuthor.wordpress.com. The pieces reflect the years spanning 2019 up to the beginning of 2025. I decided to categorize in chapters reflecting the beginnings, middles, and endings which encompass our lives. From the changing of seasons in nature to the changes in our lifetimes, and the *seasons* of growth we experience within ourselves, our families, communities, etc. The subject matter varies and touches on all aspects of our humanness, our individuality, family, community, our ever-changing world, personal growth, and more. All told through my own experiences. Although there is poetry in the book, this book differs from my other publications, every title is not necessarily poetry, but each does have a poetic voice throughout.

How was the title born; you may be wondering.

I live in a community where of late several of our neighbors have become owners of chickens and roosters. The chickens are basically quiet, but the roosters are well - LOUD. Nearly every morning while I'm sipping my morning coffee, penning my blog posts, I hear an orchestra of rooster calls in the distance. It seemed a fitting perfect title. I hope you enjoy –

The Rooster Diaries.

Endings always lead to beginnings.

1
BEGINNINGS

Opening a Door to NEW

Today I woke up late *and* still sick. Which I have been the entire weekend. I have conceded to the fact that I needed some down time, and I am extremely grateful that it happened this weekend and not the previous (Christmas).

Still, New Years Day, not going to be a *perfect* start (says the perfectionist in me). But I remind myself that it is a START. Another new day. Another new year. Another *chance* to start anew. A new beginning can be had at every moment you take a breath, simply because you have been given the gift of TAKING A BREATH.

So, Happy New Year to ME. I will start anew, simply because I still breathe. I will do my best every day to be the best ME I can be and rather than making all kinds of resolutions to be a different me, instead this new year I resolve to respect the person I have grown to be and simply accept me for ME.

In Closing

Growing into me hasn't been easy. I had to stop believing what was - told about me and start to believe in what I know about me.

We are once again at the end of another year.
This year brought and took many things, as most every year does.

It brought my Big Six OH birthday, the passing year taking with it a little more of my youth.
And at the same time, it brought many beautiful wishes from so many wonderful people that I am blessed to have in my life, opening my eyes to how grateful I am to be alive.

It added weight, not only to my frame - but also to what my shoulders could take, a few more lines for my worries to call home.

Resilience tested ripped.
Strength broke.
With seeds of faith sown, courage could once again grow.

But the best it brought was the most blessed event and abounding joy I could have ever hoped for — a baby to love and adore!

A Grandson.

A healthy birth despite the early arrival. A healthy mom despite numerous health trials. A new appreciation for gifts of service given by total strangers to help ease the journey we must travel.

The realization that I am loved, missed, appreciated, and needed.

The pride of accomplishment of trying a lot of NEW and learning I can do things I thought I could never DO.

Sadness and relief to finally accept some things - at the cross-they must be left. I can only do so much before exhaust replaces resolve. There is nothing left for my heart to do but trust.

Hope for a better tomorrow for those we love who continue to stumble over the same hurdles over and over. A replenishing of hope lost from disappointments we have suffered when we've given our most hope to those who continue to abuse it.

And when our dedication is tested to the breaking point by remaining in a constant state of bent. Mothers are human. And as we age, our emotional backbones become brittle. We lose the *marrow* needed to cushion the blows. Compassion does not show where our faith has lost room to grow and where our hope has nowhere to go. We lose our flexible minds when we are confused by other's actions, time after time.

Prayer is the only thing saving our compassionate, empathetic hearts from becoming empty vaults, too. Though our love remains eternal, we only have so much patience to spend on those who choose to abuse.

I pray the new year upon us will be the one that holds the cure for those of us who suffer, who still have more to learn, whose eyes have not yet opened to some of the most obvious but to them still deeply buried clues.

Families can be whole so peace can finally grow in a world that has neglected so many and embraced so few.

The years are passing us by, and we continue to grow old. Too precious is time for it to not be spent wisely, for so much of it has been long sold.

So let us heed the truth told.

Twenty-Twenty Four is a leap year, so we are already given an extra day to make it the most promising to achieve a well-needed change.

Kindness is a simple wisdom to embrace. Give it a try at every exchange.

Sending all my Peace, Love, and Cheer.
I wish you all a Merry Christmas and an even better New Year.

My Word for the New Year

Is NEW

I realize that may sound a bit strange, but I don't mean NEW in the often approach of - *out with the old, in with the new.*

NO. In this new year (2023), I'm hoping there will be a real focus on NEW. In terms of *opening* myself rather than *hiding behind* beliefs, limits, and the mundane.

Basically, to stop the usual protocol of always doing the same and try working in a little or hopefully a lot more - NEW.

Try incorporating a few new habits. Take some new routes when running errands. Try a new recipe here and there. Rather than tea with the evening spread, have a glass of wine instead. You get the gist of it.

Even a little bit of NEW can make a huge difference in our *inner* worldview. It's refreshing. It sparks motivation. It gets those creative juices flowing and causes a rise in our karmic vibration.

So this year, my focus will be NOT on losing excess weight. NOT on checking off every household To Do, NOT to make any monumental life change, but instead to venture off the regular tried and true by adding a little more - NEW.

If at First You Don't Succeed

Try and try again.

I have deduced that my life is a series of start overs.

I am forever climbing back on the horse; crawling back into the wagon; picking myself up by the bootstraps and starting again - over and over and over.

But at least I am not remaining face down in the muck of it all and giving up.

At least I do start over; and over *and over*.

Better to fail (if you want to call it that, I prefer the word try) than to never have tried. To never attempt a better way, to never look for ways of improving.

To never have to start over means you never gave anything a try. I am sure no human has succeeded in their every attempt at everything.

So, starting over is the main ingredient to a fully realized life. There must be a series of start overs to continue our journey, lest we find ourselves stuck in the muck, unable to get up. Now that would certainly mean our demise.

So, I am all for lots and lots and lots of tries.

Seize the Day, Your Way

You can either waste today

Or you can embrace today

Be the person you see in your dreams

Be your authentic - *ME*

Cracks

We come into this world with all kinds of surface cracks

Over time the weight of the world causes those cracks to deepen

Those cracks become wounds that harden over time but never heal

Until we take the time to peel back the scars of every single wound

Apply ointment

A healing salve

Wisdom, mercy, love

The balm of the Healer

Jesus

Only He can administer what our wounds need

He is the glue that will mend those cracks from the inside out

Over time our characters bloom

Our cracks become the most intricate, beautiful details of our lives

A map tracing our journey

Giving purpose to the breaks that caused them

They are the paths to the depths of our hearts

Letting your spirit peek from the inside out

Giving the world a glimpse at who you really are

Through the cracks lies the meaning of our lives

Jesus is the glue that keeps us from falling apart

He keeps our hearts from shattering from the cracks

He makes us strong despite our lack

Jesus, show me the beauty

Through every single crack

That make up who I am

New Year Revolution

Of SELF

No to

Sugar

Processed

Simple carbs

Yes to

Slimmer

Healthier

Body

No to

Staying up too late

Yes to

Feeling better

Better mood

Stronger immunity

Glowing skin

No to

Putting off the things you want to do for you

Yes to

More joy

Fulfillment

Rewarding sense of accomplishment

No to

People who want to siphon your energetic field of protection

Yes to

Freedom to be the person you were born to be

No to

Other people's dramas

Yes to

Your own peaceful calm

No to

Self-sabotaging beliefs, thoughts, and impulses

Yes to

Living your authentic life

No to

Stagnant repeat of years gone by

Yes to

REVOLUTION

New year

Same you

In a Better Frame of

Life

Blue Swayed, Shoes

If you feel stuck in your shoes and unable to move, know that you can take your feet out of the shoes you are wearing. You know, those old worn-out ones that never really fit quite right.

Your shoes are stuck, not you. Step out of them and move. The choice has always been there. It's the moving that's up to you.

Whoever chose those shoes, should learn to walk in their own a little better before choosing for you, before stepping on toes not their own.

It's time to give 'em the boot.

Stop letting your mood be swayed into blue.

Step into a new pair of shoes.

Boxed

When we confine ourselves to live our lives *inside of the box* (figuratively speaking) we remain stuck. Inside the box we only see out through the windows our fears have left undraped. Our view of the world around us is limited. With our focus narrowed we miss the door that's right there in front of us. It stands waiting for us to grasp the knob and turn.

With the door open we can see the whole picture from a different view entirely.

We miss so much when we remain stuck in our boxes.

Beyond our draped mind lies a world full of opportunities. All we must do is turn the knob, open the door, and step out of our box.

It's Monday

If you had a relaxing weekend, that's great. If you had a weekend that, has you muttering this Monday morning... "What weekend?" Well to that I would say I am with you, sort of, but probably for different reasons.

I am the type of person who, *(and this is only for myself mind you)*, believes that all the things - household, etc. - that you cannot accomplish Monday through Friday, should and MUST be accomplished on the weekend.

This philosophy of course leaves virtually no room for rest, as the - *things to do list* - is certainly always insurmountable. So, on the rare times that I do divulge in actual weekend rest time, I usually begin my Mondays with "What weekend? because I didn't spend it *working* and did spend it resting.

Make sense? Probably only to a few likeminded individuals who enjoy working.

I guess the better way to look at this is how one defines "work". If working (getting things accomplished) on the home front brings about a sense of joy and relaxation to you, then that time would be considered at least with the result, restful.

If you are working your fingers to the bones on the weekend doing the menial, though necessary chores out of a sense of obligation and/or because other household members *are* resting, then I would suggest you follow them around and take notes. Because the whole purpose of time-off of your day job, whether it be on the weekend or during the week, is to replenish, rejuvenate, AKA REST your body, mind, and spirit. To feed your soul with the fruits (activities) that bring you joy. Which other family members are obviously doing.

For myself a truly restful weekend consists of a combination of work *and* rest. After all it is a great feeling to sit down for tea in a cozy, clean area of the house that you just blessed with a quick sweep and dust. And to sit an enjoy a cup of tea in that room surely brings one to a most restful place indeed.

That is the type of time-off that best suits me.

So, the next time I am spending my days off doing anything other than the above mentioned, I vow to take notepad and pencil in hand, and quickly find, and follow, the first person I see that is.

After all, if we are going to wake up Monday morning with the lingering thought of "what weekend", when someone asks us how ours was, it may as well be for the right reasons.

Our definition of *rest*.
Which for some of us has a little bit of work thrown in for good measure.

Notions, Yearnings, and Choices

When the spirit moves - get up and DO.

I can't even begin to count the number of times I've gotten a notion, a yearning, even a churning in my gut to embark on something fun. A thought comes to mind to spend the day exploring an activity that would involve something I really love to do, like my writing and art.

The idea no sooner enters my mind and before I am even aware, I am shutting the notion right down with the usual...*yes but I really need, or rather, should, work on - this or that.* With *this or that* almost always being something which would benefit someone (or more precisely *everyone*) other than - ME.

Am I alone here or are there others out there who do the exact same thing?

I say let's stop!

And let's start acting on those notions.

Indulging those yearnings.

And making choices to DO the things that the person to benefit most from, is YOU.

We are responsible for our happiness so let's choose to make ourselves happy.

Let's do those things that make our tummies flutter with excitement.

That make our eyes sparkle with anticipation.

That brings smiles to our mouths that reach all the way up to the corners of our eyes.

And that fill us with JOY.

Next time you wake up and a notion pops into your mind - follow it all the way through to the DO.

Make a choice for YOU.
And I will too.

Wellness Priorities

Begin with taking care of self

Spend time silently to connect with that from which you came

We are of God and He is within us

Stretch and exercise our bodies

Our physical state is important too

In optimal form it allows us to do the things we ought to do

Be present with family

Be energetic in your chores

Days just seem to run smoother when you take that little extra time to -

Make the bed

Wash the dish

Sweep up the dust from the floor -

All the necessary tasks

To live well and to thrive

Make your wellness a priority

Well body, soul, and mind

Moon Wink

The moon is still visible

But the sun is peeking its bright

Another beautiful morning awakes after a calm and restful night

The sand feels warm against my bottom as I prepare to meditate

I close my eyes and with my vision in mind

to the sky I gaze

I hear the rise of the ocean's wave

after a gentle kiss to its shore,

Her nature in harmony with my breath

The breeze tickles past my cheek

The temperature just right

Another beautiful morn awakes from her restful night

And thus, a new year awakens

To another beautiful morn

Another year filled with hope

Another chance to stand together

Shoulder to shoulder

Hand in hand

Unity for every woman, child, and man

The past has fallen away

No longer holding old issues over head

Old wounds heal

Broken hearts mend

When we look to each other not as foe but as friend

Our lives can be peace filled again

Differing views are heard

No problems warrant harsh words

A new year wakes as we embark on a new age

Embrace a new concept to live a new way

As the moon gives a wink at the start of new day

One Word

No THREE

Last year my word for 2020 was "Release", and it too was the moral of my 2020 story.

This year when "my word" came to me, two others followed. So, my goal is to live this year with the focus on all three. Leading with the word INTENTIONAL (and the two companion words are Attainable and Reality).

So, my WORD for 2021 is INTENTIONAL - and
The belief system fueling my new year is going to be - In all my thoughts and actions I will strive to live **intentionally**, by doing so all my goals are **attainable** and will be my **reality**.

I believe, for myself at least, to live intentionally (or *with intention*, is to live everyday with my bigger picture in clear view. Not necessarily to be focused ON the bigger picture, as then my focus would be away from the present moment, which I believe (for myself at least), is where I most need to improve to see myself arriving at the bigger picture.

So, I will, *with intention*, live every moment of the day believing that all I set my mind to is attainable and will be my reality. When? - is not for me to know. But one thing I do know is, if my thoughts don't align with my desires and my actions don't compliment those thoughts and desires in some actionable way, each day, then the obvious answer will be NEVER, to the question of WHEN?

Now it's your turn. Pick a word. Any word. Let it propel your mind to a new realm of thinking. Let it motivate your body to a new level of action. And let it take you further than you have ever traveled before on the road to *your* bigger picture where all *your* dreams become *your* reality.

So, pick one...or if you need, two or even three.

Happy 2021!!!

And the Universe Says

GO FOR IT!

Stop being depleted. It's time to get deployed.
Go into action doing what you enjoy. What have you got to lose, but time?

If you don't DO what you were put on this planet to do, which is being the best version of YOU, you'll never touch the hearts that are yearning.

Your thread in the tapestry will never be woven all the way through. It will forever be left dangling. The universe left waiting, for all that is YOU.

Everybody knows their purpose. It's told to us by that little voice that screams "yippie" when we're actively chasing our dreams. Some just fail to listen, and that's when dreams slip away.

We can see them in the distance, but they seem ungraspable through a veil.

Reach deep inside where your true self, likes to hide and pull away the curtain of fear and doubt. DO what makes your little voice shout.

After all that's what this life is really all about.

History Repeats Itself

AS DO I...

I have heard it said that history repeats itself. Well apparently, so do I.

Last year at this time I began writing in a journal. I didn't begin at the beginning though, which astounds me. I am a little on the OCD side and so starting in the middle of the month, in the middle of a journal, well let's just say it is out of my norm. But I DID. And what do you suppose I wrote about? The exact issues I am STILL dealing with. The exact habits that I am (and apparently was) trying to break or change. So, do you mean to tell me that in a whole entire year I have made no progress at all?

No, I have made progress. I'm still riding the horse. I am writing in the very journal, *which by the way I only wrote in twice last year,* and I have written in it now for nearly an entire month. So yes, I have and continue to make progress. Because there is no real finish line with self-discovery, self-awareness, with growing, and becoming, and being oneself. It's an ongoing practice. And the only way to not make progress is to not keep at it.

So YES, history does repeat itself and so do we. Until we get it right. We keep trying. We keep changing. We keep evolving.

As for me, I will continue to keep mounting the horse, fall off, dust off, and RIDE AGAIN.

I hope you'll do the same.

Serenity – This Way

Serenity Found

The path to serenity follows in the same direction as the *road to happiness*, the road, *less traveled* by so many. Stuck behind the many roadblocks we build, which skew our vision of a horizon that is open to all who *choose* to see it.

I'm finding my New Year journey is taking me down avenues I have scarcely ventured before. In the little alleyways that make up my thought patterns, I am discovering so many times that I took the detour rather than plowing right through. I assumed the roadblock was to shield me from extreme danger. But it turns out there was just a little bump in the road that I could easily manage to pass over.

When fear tells me to STOP, I will yield, only to assess the situation, then with my COURAGE in gear - I will KEEP GOING to see what lies ahead.

So Far So Good

Here we are nearly two weeks into this New Year and so far, so good. Although my body has begun it with a bronchial virus, the rest of me is feeling quite well. Usually, I go into a new year with a whole bunch of changes I plan on making to myself, my life, my house, my habits...and the list goes on. And although my intentions are always very sincere about *two hours* into the new year, I hear that familiar tiny voice shouting "you're not going to do it!", "you're not going to do it!", "you're not going to do it!".

And ultimately it always proves right. So, this year before the chant began, I hollered back "WRONG!", and I decided to turn over a new attitude instead of a new leaf. Rather than turning the page to a new chapter in the same book I decided to shelve that one and open a fresh new read.

Well so far not only do I NOT hear the shouts of that tiny critic's voice, but I can see my inner fan jumping up and down, waving me on and praising "You're doing it!" and "Keep it up!"

So, what is the difference between this year and every other year? Why is the start seeming to go right, rather than wrong, or better said, in the same direction? To be honest, I'm not sure but I suspect it has something to do with a little bit of everything. My age for one. I'm just too old to keep up the same pace of getting nowhere. I seem to be moving faster and faster to the same old spot I wind up every year. Frankly the closer I get to my finish line the more I want to finish with a bang, rather than a flop. So, the work must be done, and so this year I think I have *really begun*.

Well, now I don't want to jinx myself here so I will stop. After all, I want my momentum to continue, and yes, I do believe that a certain amount of *overconfidence* can be a jinx. I will finish by saying this...

I suspect that every other year I have started with a mental attitude that I was going to BE a different person just because I thought I needed to BE different. This year I am not fooling myself by thinking I can be a different person. I was born and will always be ME. So, with a bit more enlightenment, I'm feeling good about just remaining the same person trying to do things in a little *different* way because the old ways simply don't seem to work (at least not for me).

So, this year (at least for almost two weeks into it), I'm being myself, I'm accepting myself, and I'm excited and open to whatever the universe has in store for ME, and I am feeling confident that I can and *will* handle every aspect (whether good or not so good), with gratitude and joy.

Hey that's it, that's the answer...Gratitude and Joy, just to BE.

Hanging on by a Thread is Still Hanging On
Tying Up Loose Ends

It's January and at our house, January is an extremely lean month. There is not much wiggle room where finances are concerned. Not only is it right after Christmas but we have our biggest bill due in January. So, in addition to all the other hats, this mom wears on a *regular* month, in January the "Financial Planner Guru", "Circus (*money*) Juggler", and "Stretch a Penny Armstrong" hats all get to be worn simultaneously.

So today, being Saturday, a day off work and a day for household responsibilities, I have a task or two. Pay the rest of the month's bills that MUST be paid and do the grocery shopping with what's left. WHAT'S LEFT? There isn't even enough for phase one of this assignment. How on earth am I going to manage? Creativity is KEY. And determination. As well as *you got no choice girl, just do it!*

Now I could have gotten all glum and defeated and adopted the poor me attitude, but instead, I put on my big girl pants, rolled up my sleeves and got to work on it. First, I started pooling from every available resource. Second, I planned. What is needed? What can we NOT live without? Who, (or in the case of groceries) what, can wait? Then began, systematically to tackle the tasks at hand.

Fast forward a few hours... With all my responsibilities complete I feel great. I did it! I made all my ends meet, no matter how frayed they were when I began. I find it invigorating to have to "make do". To pull out my domestic bag of tricks and let the creativity flow. There is always a way if there is a will, is what I have always said. No matter how tattered those ends, with a plan, anything can be tackled and with conviction, anything can be achieved.

Self-discipline is something I have been lacking lately and now I am reaping what I have sown. But that's OK because everyone needs a little adjusting occasionally, no one is perfect, and we all fall into a *comfortable zone* where we walk blindly along not seeing the red flags waving ferociously in our peripheral vision.

As always, my motto remains, if there is a will, there is a way, and today I proved it *again*.

And I am learning that...

To ensure your ends will meet, you must stop wasting the string.

Turn the Key
Opening the Door to NEW

The thought of living yet another year in the same fashion as every other that has passed makes me want to double over onto my knees and simply give up. So, I have taken to a new practice, one that I planned to begin last year on January 1st but didn't. The practice I have begun is that I am learning and studying to live a more wellness centered life. I crave balance. Freedom from the merry-go-round, same old spin I have lived my whole life. A constant mad dash to get nowhere, no further, certainly no better off. Year after year I start the same old way, and I end it in the same place I began it. Never getting ahead. Never feeling anything but defeated. There must be something more meaningful that energizes a soul to awake every day excited to live it. I am not sure I have ever had that kind of motivation or energy. Life, as I have been living it only drains me of energy, and it does not sustain me in the least. Not emotionally, not spiritually, and not financially.

I am learning to free myself of the chains that keep me bound to that merry-go-round way of living. I realize I hold the keys that lock those chains in place, but I often freely give those keys to others to hold. I also hold the keys that unlock those chains. The difference is that I am the only one with the power to use those keys. So, freedom to live the life I crave is mine - I need only turn the key.

2
SPRING

Crucify

I hope that I would be the Veronica had I lived in the time of Christ.

To wipe the sweat and tears from the face of a Holy Man, they sacrificed.

I hope that I would be the Good Samaritan who helped carry a cross,

for a Holy Man whose garments were torn and tossed.

I hope that I would have the faith of a Mother whose son they beat,

then placed a crown of thorns upon His Holy Head,

and left in a dungeon to bleed.

I hope I would not have taken part with those who sentenced a Holy Man to His death.

Who stood and watched the Son of God, take His final breath.

But in my saddened heart I know - as a sinner surely, I was.

I am no better now than any of those were then.

Those who left a Holy Man for dead.

Had I been alive in the time of Jesus the Christ.

Surely, I, as the sinner I am, would have screamed along with the crowd -

Crucify, crucify, crucify - this Man,

Whose death gave eternal life.

And after 2000 plus years later,

It seems nothing has changed with the crowd or with, I.

For to the *unalike* - we still cry,

Crucify, crucify, CRUCIFY!

Spring

Every day is a chance to begin again.

Renew.

Reset.

Rejuvenate.

Reinvent.

The birds chirp and gleefully greet another day.

The rooster crowing offers us an audible nudge to wake.

Crisp, clear springtime air,

It cozily tickles my neck.

As I settle myself near an open window,

allowing a breeze to clear cobwebs,

from my foggy head.

Recharge my soul.

Ready my mind.

To start again.

Clearing my thoughts from yesterday's chatter,

still pricking at me to fret.

What will the new day bring?

I am excited about anything!

I can't wait to see what other treasures I may get.

The gift opened along with my eyes.

Blessed was I when my body did rise,

From the bed, I was blessed – for rest.

The break of day – a reminder,

I am ALIVE to begin again.

With praise and gratitude,

I cheer an exuberant,

AMEN!

Today is the First Day of Spring

The Spring Equinox signifies the beginning of a new season, the season of life.

Mother Nature gently beckons her planet earth that it's time to awake from winter's slumber and dormant state. Although, old man winter's chill lingers in the air. The promise of Spring's warmer days is today, officially here!

Although all four seasons affect me artistically, I find springtime nudges my creative senses to awaken with a little more vigor than summer, fall, or winter. Just as the cool rain cleanses the palate of Earth, enriching the soil to nourish its seedlings of new life, the emergence of Spring is an enrichment to my artist's heart, bringing a sense of wonder and joy to my life.

Is it any wonder that the cosmos, in its magnificence and the ebb and flow of seasons, influences us, mind, body, and spirit? Just look up at the night sky and feel your creative senses twinkle. Feel your heart burst as you gaze up at the bright fullness of the moon against the backdrop of a dark, deep-blue night sky.

My word for the year is NEW, and so far, I have been changing things up in my life, though subtly, to embrace and encourage NEW whenever the opportunity unfolds.

The beginning of Spring is a perfect time to begin a *new* habit.

Enjoy the stillness of a cool spring morning, take in the sunshine, and bless your day with time to meditate. Meditation -

like the spring rains, cleanses our minds and nourishes us to be open to the newness of life every day.

Astrologically, we have this week a NEW MOON to look forward to. This month the new moon is in the sign of Aries, which signifies new beginnings (Aries being the first sign of the zodiac).

Enjoy and embrace - the first day of spring IS today!

And All That Jazz

Step into my ballroom.

Take a twirl with me.

Let's see what fate has in store.

Why not live our destiny?

Tomorrow is not a given,

Today is all we have.

Let's take a chance on living,

And all that -

jazz.

Have a Beautiful Day

Despite the gloom

Despite the rain

We hold enough light within ourselves

To push through clouds that hang

To calm the moods that sway

Especially on the gloomy days

So be the sunshine

Spread your light

Have a beautiful day

Despite

Is it Not Enough That I Bled?

So that you might have life instead

Still my Fathers children remain in despair

Remain fighting wars

Continue pouring Satan's poison in my sores

Yet I forgive and love them more

Is it not enough that I bled

Yet there remains on earth many still unfed

Many whom are not being clothed

Many who call an alley - home

Those that simply look away

Refusing to care for my sheep

Cause the wounds I've sustained for them

to bleed

Earth Day

We think the Earth belongs to us.

The earth belongs to no man.

Beautiful Earth open and plentiful with precious resources,

Shares them with us

And we thank her by ravaging and destroying those resources,

Including ourselves

We divide and conquer her land,

Brutally raping her precious soil of its minerals.

Leaving her plush forests leveled,

To honor our gods of development.

We think the Earth belongs to us.

We think we have the right.

We think the answer to every problem,

Is to give up *right*,

Take up *wrong*,

Ammo up armies to fight.

We think that others belong to us.

Should follow as we'd like.

We think that *freedom* is for sale.

Man's merchandise.

No!

Freedom is a God-given right.

Today darkness befalls humankind,

Where once light shined.

Dimmed in the shadow of a world,

Easiest to navigate,

While pretending to be blind.

And our neighbors are being shot.

And countries are being bombed.

All within plain sight.

Reasoning has escaped.

Common sense gone.

Chaos replaced law,

A long time ago.

From their delusion,

Men decide,

There is only one way in which to exist.

So, commence to put up fist,

To those who disagree,

To those who choose to resist.

Debating what is a *human* right,

When one's choice is,

You must die,

Another loses,

Their choice for life.

Differing opinions,

Opposite beliefs,

Conflict ensues,

If not in agreement,

With *me*.

And in those lands choosing to be FREE,

Their women are stripped of purity.

Their children have lost their safety.

Robbed of home,

Murdered at school,

Safe places? No such spaces.

Under the new RULE.

Images of tears and blank stares on faces,

Tattooed on brains and in hearts.

All remnants of their past - gone.

Their present - is hell on earth.

A Future - is unimaginable,

For terror is all they can see.

But the brave continues to fight.

They lost their *choice* for peace.

They lost their *God-given* right.

Because of one man's false truth.

Because one man decided,

To ammo his armies to fight.

He must think he has the right.

He must think the Earth belongs to him.

Someone should inform him,

She does not!

Precious Earth belongs to NO MAN.

And neither does the children of God.

When man's decisions are bent to destroy,

He no longer will need his armies deployed,

On a planet left barren and void.

It's Just Routine

Yes, it is important to have routines. To have at least an outline of how you're going to fill the hours of the day. But if you're too rigid about it, it can cause your funny bone to break.

That same stability that you so desperately try to establish with your many routines, is the very component that will cause your structure to fall apart.

You must allow for some wiggle room to be able to enjoy the day as it flows. You must be open for a quick change if the opportunity should arise. That's what brings us the most joy in our lives.

The unexpected visit from a friend, that leaves you gasping for air as you laugh for hours reminiscing through the past.

Those "drop everything days" for outings that were anything but planned.

The weekends when you do nothing but binge watch, read, and feast.

All these scenarios are what humans occasionally need. Leaving your day open to enjoy those "whatever's" that come along, gives us the momentum to be able to stick to our outlines. I mean if you think about it, an outline is just a loose draft of what is to be. It is meant to be changed as the story unfolds. Its changeability is so the lives of the characters can better be told. And so, it is with the outlines of our days and the routines we set in place.

Sure, it's a great feeling to get everything you set out to do - done. To be able to check off all the little boxes, but I wouldn't trade anything for those seemingly untimely occasions when everything went awry - because those are the days etched in memory that turned out to be the best days of my life.

Because we all need a break from our rigid routines. To do lists are great, but sometimes we must place our check marks outside of the little boxes to enjoy more than what's on our plates.

My advice - routines are a YES. Sticking to them, SURE, but remember to leave a little wiggle room so LIFE can unfold, and when it does - Go with the FLOW.

To do list

_____ whatever should come along - CHECK

Tree of Life

THE DAY THE HEART OF GOD HUNG UPON A TREE * TO SET US FREE
I EXTEND TO YOU MY WISDOM * WHICH NOURISHES FROM THE ROOT * TO PLACE A
SOLID GROUND * UNDERNEATH YOUR SLIPPERY FOOT * I CAME TO YOU A TREE OF
LIFE * BUT TO A WOUNDED PEOPLE I WAS MET WITH STRIFE * AND FROM THEIR OWN
INFLICTION * THEY IN TURN WOUNDED ME * MY FATHER'S PLAN * WAS WHAT I HAD
COME TO TEACH * I COMMUNICATED MY PURPOSE * IN UNIVERSAL SPEECH * BUT TO
A PEOPLE WHOSE EARS WERE DEAF TO TRUTH * AND SELF-RIGHTEOUS FALLACIES
KEPT THEM BLIND * TO WISDOM'S KNOWLEDGE * THEY WERE NOT INCLINED * AND TO
PARTAKE IN THE TREE OF LIFE * THEY DECLINED * THEIR MADNESS FUELED * THE
FLAMES OF HELL UNLEASHED * FOR THEIR SINS * TO BE RELEASED * WITH THEIR
STRAPS * MY TRUNK WAS SLASHED * AN INFERNO OF THEIR ANGER SEETHED * THE
DAY THEY PLOTTED * TO NAIL ME TO A TREE * UNWILLING TO LISTEN
THEY CHOSE INSTEAD * TO PIERCE MY SIDE * TO SEE IF I LAY DEAD
THEIR ANGER * TO FORCE THE HEAVENS TO SHAKE * THEIR VILE
TO CAUSE THE EARTH TO QUAKE * THE ANGELS IN UNISON
CRIED THAT DAY * AS THE TRUMPETS ROARED * WITH EVERY
DRIVEN NAIL * IN THEIR FURY OF IGNORANCE AND PRIDE
THEY STRETCHED MY ARMS TO OPEN WIDE
AND THOUGH BATTERED, SCARRED AND BRUISED
FOREVERMORE REMAIN OPEN FOR YOU
THE HEAVENS SHOOK * A SAMARITAN LOOKED
AS THE CROSS WAS CARRIED * ANGELS CRYING
ALONGSIDE MARY * BLACKENED CLOUDS
OF JUSTICE ENCOMPASSED THOSE THERE
THEIR OWN CRUEL HEARTS * GRIPPED
IN FEAR * AS THE LOVING HEART OF GOD
LAY BARE * THE FAITHLESS THAT
GAVE THEIR SOULS AWAY * THEIR SINS
HE ALSO FORGAVE THAT DAY
NOW IN SHAME * THEY COULD
NO LONGER BEAR TO LOOK
THE DAY THE WORLD SILENTLY
STOOD STILL * UNDER HEAVENS
THAT SHOOK * THAT DAY A TREE
WAS CARRIED * AND THE ROLE
OF CROSS WAS BOUGHT * OUR SINS
HE CLAIMED * HE TOOK WITH HIM
OUR BLAME * FROM THE FONT
OF HIS MERCY * NEW LIFE
SPRUNG FORTH * MAN'S DEATH
CONQUERED * HIS SINS ABORT
THE DAY THE WORLD WAS
STRICKEN STILL * HE WHISPERED
NOT MINE * BUT MY FATHER'S
WILL * HIS FINAL BREATH
EXHALED * GOD'S KINGDOM
PREVAILED * FROM THE BONDAGE
OF DEATH * WE ARE SET FREE
IN US NEW LIFE * HE BREATHES*
HIS MERCY CAN NEVER BE SPENT*
HE BOUGHT US FREEDOM
FROM OUR OWN DEATH
BORN TO TEACH, TO LOVE,
TO DIE * HE REMAINS FOR US
THE TREE OF LIFE

A POEM BY HOLLY COOP

Happy Easter Monday

We are into a new season (Spring), a new month (April), and with Christ's Resurrection (Alleluia!) new LIFE (Today).

As a Christian, I find it so comforting to know that, *as children of God*, we are forgiven time and time again for our wrongs. Christ made sure of this by giving up His own life for ours, on the cross.

We can trust that our shortcomings can be opportunities for learning and our mistakes don't have to destroy us. Rather they can be the fuel that serves to deploy us into action, to do better.

If, at times we find ourselves caught in a familiar loop where our actions stunt our goals rather than propel them forward, we can remind ourselves that every day is a chance to begin the baby steps that will help us practice new routines that will serve our lives better.

We can do all this with the knowledge that when we fail, we are not failures. We are explorers, looking in different directions to find our way. When at times we feel lost, we can be reminded that taking a variety of avenues to get where we want to be, doesn't mean our compasses are off, *necessarily*. If we are enjoying the scenery along the way, it's all good, everything is OK.

And when life takes its toll and blue colors our mood. We can keep our peace as we muddle through, because faith gives us the promise that there is *always* a rainbow at the end of the blue. And beyond the clouds there is a silver lining that adorns our every mood.

For me, Easter is a reminder of all this.

As I, with age have grown a little wiser, I have found it a blessing to expand my understanding of various religious beliefs and what I have learned is that when we allow ourselves to look at faith through a wider lens, we see more similarities than differences.

We are all born with a moral compass within us. We may follow different paths. We may have different elements that make up our individual maps, but the destination is the same.

You don't have to be a Christian to have a better sense of hope and a stronger feeling of joy -
When the morning breaks with the sound of chirping birds. When we are blessed to have the daylight stretched, to enjoy the warmth of sun, and to close the day by giving thanks to the night sky, with all its stars twinkling above.

Buds peeking from branches of trees. The ground, brown from winters death, suddenly transformed to green -
On this Easter Monday I give thanks for all of these and I'm looking forward to - A new season (Spring), a new month (April), and with Christ's Resurrection (Alleluia!) a new LIFE (Today).

Put Your Joy On

Every single morning especially when mood is down
Reach deep into your heart of hearts
And put that JOY back on

When in the wee hours
Depression lurks
Count your blessings
Say a prayer
Surrender your cares to the universe

When the sun rises, and your day must begin
Try to remember a frown steals more energy
Than ever does a grin

Joy is like a garment you must dress yourself with each day, to
ensure your spirit be protected from the weathering of life
And just as your skin is cocooned with protection by the wearing
of slacks and shirts, keeping you warm and dry from the
climates of the earth -

Joy can be a protection from the harsh elements *of life*
It will cocoon your spirit from those who often shower a sunny
day with the gloom from their drama and strife

Before your toes even hit the floor
Thank your God for another morn
If your lips are tightly pressed into a frown
And in conflicting direction your mind seems torn
Stand up tall stand up straight
Make a conscious decision to step away

From all past mistakes
And then put your JOY on

With feelings frayed
Patience strained
And YES, if you must then do it afraid
But put that joy right on

Your light on this earth is meant to shine
Don't let any darkness from this world dim your spark
When blinded by the fog of depression
The only visible light is that which beams from your heart
Let it stream in to uncover depression's dark

When your eyes are opened from the night's sleep
Joy, it's not always the feeling *there* to greet
It doesn't appear magically for some
A great majority of people must reach far to put their joy on

So, reach
As far as the universe is deep

What have you got to lose
Except precious time for your light to shine
While your star is beaming here on earth

Learn from the many stars - *souls passed on*
Their lights beam bright from above
It's because while they were here, they kept their joy put on
Now from the Heavens their joy shines on us

And we can see twinkling, when we look into the eyes of the ones, we are lucky to love

Those are the reasons for you
To *keep* your JOY put on

Chicago Style

Birds flutter around
Not sure what to do

White has covered the ground
that normally provides their food

The branches they planned to rest upon
too slippery for their feet to hang on

Tis the Season in Chicagoland...
Where the question remains
Is it Spring?
Summer?
Winter?
Or fall?

...The only place where in one single day
We can experience, them all.

3
PLANTING SEEDS

Karma Happy

Your peeps should lift you up, not let you down.

It doesn't take much, a simple word

a gentle smile

Every little bit can help

If the request is but an inch

Offer a mile

The karma is yours that will make its way round

Be a peep that lifts up

not one that lets down

Be

Karma Happy

A Character Flaw or a Spirit, Broken?

Why all these things
that has happened to me
Why have you allowed to be
Is it a test to prove
I will be devoted to you
I pray that I do
I hope that my heart remains unhardened

The last two upheavals
I thought more than I could bear
Each had characteristics
Something personal that would shake me to my core
Knock me off my horse
Where I thought the ride was smooth

But you saw me through the roughness
To a place where I could learn
And so I survived doing the best I could do
And yes, you granted us the most mercy we could have ever known
For which I will be forever grateful and in awe

But this time Lord
This time
You might as well have lit the match
than if the Devil had himself
To set my flesh on fire
While watching my heart melt

My brain may tell me to run and stop relying on humankind
There is too much hurt in this world
I think I would rather die
I may never understand the reason for this; my worst day ever
A title I gave each that passed and thought they would be the last
Never say never
But here I face again
Another course of dread
Will it never end

I no sooner get back up on that horse
Steer my attention towards another course
My stomach kicked again
My breath exits my lungs
Dizziness fills my head
Another jolt I must face
How many lessons must I learn
At least I have the calm, cool of your grace
To comfort me through the burn

I pray this be the last of my life's lessons class
that I am required to attend
As my strength and wits near their end
But then I may be a pile of dust
In the bottom of an urn
And only as I cross through the gate
will I know
if *sufficient*, were the lessons learned

How Brilliant is Your Light?

You hear it on the news shows,

from strangers on the street,

at home from a family where opinions aren't refrained,

and even from the thoughts that accumulate in your brain.

The complaints about the shape this world is in

and how we will never see the good days again.

Well, *we* live in this world.

And even though the world can be a real shit hole

no matter the conditions that surround,

WE must live as the light.

WE must BE the light.

And the brighter our light,

the more difficult it is for evil and evil doers

to penetrate that light.

Imagine a world where every human being's light is shining at its brightest.

What would that do to the darkness of the world?

There would be none.

Darkness would vanish.

Evil would not survive

in a world of pure light.

So next time you find yourself complaining/ranting

about the shit-hole state of the world

and everything not right,

look deep into your heart,

ask yourself the question

how brilliant is my light?

We have so many blessings in this beautiful place where we dwell.

God draws His love from the deepest of wells.

He gave us a Savior, a brother, a friend,

parables to keep us wise 'til the end.

So why do we spout excuses?

Why do we choose to live in a state that does more to prosper death,

Then shine as bright as a star?

Everything we see mirrors what we are.

What is the reflection you're casting out into the world?

Change begins with one.

Unity is only as great as its sum.

Make *your* reflection, be as bright as the, *Son*

Let's Focus on the Human

I am so grateful to be alive and part of, the human race. I wish we would do better at the HUMAN part. I know that we can. If we would bend our focus away from the race, unclench our fists and extend our reach to embrace.

And not see a difference when we look at another's face. But to acknowledge the gift of every soul is a chance for us to feel and know and *see* our Savior Jesus in *every* human's face.

The world will be a happier place. When we are a more *human* - human race.

Negative Thoughts

Trolling throughout my mind

Their infectious seed planted

By some who were unkind

My pleasant daydream story

Rewritten to please the masses

I'd like to take their fiction

And shove it up their asses

The narrative they have seeded within

Tells the story of their weakness

And their fear that I may win

Perhaps when I rightfully claim back my glory

I'll plant in them

A fable story

Leave them with negative thoughts trolling throughout *their* mind

I would except

I am not unkind

Don't Just Be a Spectator, Get IN the Game

Never leave a ball that you are responsible for in someone else's court.

Because ultimately when you do,

it usually will result in a foul

for you.

Lead Your Heart

Lead your heart to your dreams

They will manifest if you believe

Living the *secret* is key

Everything is possible for the eyes that see

With your mind free of doubt

Let your positive energy radiate out

Release it to the universe

Leaving your heart open

To receive

All that life has in store

Is in abundance

For the few who believe

When Push Comes to Shove

When push comes to me, I don't want to shove

I don't want to push either

I just want to invite for tea

Sit

Chat

Let's discuss

What's bothering you

What's weighing on me

Calm connection

Sitting out

Perhaps neither really know what *the push*

The shove

is really all about

Let's take out the iron

Smooth the wrinkles away

Save the pushing and shoving

For someone else's day

The tea is ready

Let's chat

Push the camel through the needle

Tie up our loose ends with a thread

Today is a good a day as any

To mend

I hear the whistle

It's calling out

I have a smile

To replace your pout

You can lend me your calm

When I'm boiling with shout

When push comes to shove

Let's sit this one out

The tea is ready

Pull up a seat

Let's chat

Crossing Lines

When lines are blurred it is difficult to see when they have been moved.

With a meticulously maneuvered sleight of hand,

Like during a magician's show,

Wrongs suddenly appear as rights and rights appear as wrongs.

Making TRUTH being harder for us, to know.

Our perspective gets a little less, objective,

When motivations and agendas become the gauge,

All the blurred lines,

Become to us a maze.

Unable to discern,

From all the lines, now curved,

Our society blindly navigates off course.

In a state of disillusion we backtrack, through the breadcrumbs of remorse.

Our moral compass lost,

When lines are blurred, they are easily crossed.

The Energy is Within YOU – Release It!

Resonate at the highest vibration

Wednesdays

I think of Wednesdays as the week's teeter totter.

An opportunity to be right in the middle of a week and make a choice.

If at the beginning of the week things were at a low, if you found yourself dragging bottom, decide to ride on the other side for the latter part of the week.

And if your week began on a high - focus on keeping steady that ride.

Either side, remember to enjoy the ride.

Every day is a blessing. A chance to make life the way you want it to be. Don't waste it making elaborate plans in your mind. Be quick to act or you may run out of time.

There are many seconds, minutes, hours, days, weeks, and years - don't let yours tick away. Don't just sit idle, teetering on the brink of doing all those things you plan, ponder, and over think.

Take the leap or sink.

Wednesday is a good day to make a choice.

Grading Scale

I fail every test You allow to present itself in my life.

Yet You remain with me through the calm and through the strife.

Making Your presence known,

You rise again and again.

Resurrecting in me new life.

Every sun,

Every moon,

Every star twinkling above,

Every wave that kisses the shore,

Magnify Your love.

Thank you for Your sacrifice,

For Your unceasing, unconditional love.

Thank you for the tests I've passed and for the many that I've failed,

I'm Thankful to have been graded on Your curve of grace and love.

Dreadful

The word of the day is...DREADFUL

Who says a mantra must be positive, uplifting, and full of fluff. What an exhausting expectation that could be, for some. What about the days that are simply too much to bear? How can a simple *happy word or phrase* help a soul to fare?

I believe a huge part of our experience is for us to at times, just simply to feel dreadful. And that is OK. It can be very therapeutic for us to let those poisonous fumes of frustration simmer for a while. Let them boil up and over, exploding from the vile bubbling from within. Because if we simply stuff them down, keeping a lid on what is making us frown, surely those feelings will surface another day with an ever more damaging power.

So, when a day arrives that you cannot bear to be alive, put your mind at ease. Simply put, *appease*, every awful emotion that should arise. After all life is full of good and bad. That should not come as a surprise. Sometimes feeling dreadful is but another needed lesson of our lives.

Be Golden

No matter how badly people treat me, I try to treat them the way they would want to be treated, rather than the way they deserve.

I choose to treat them better because that is what defines my character you see. Just as theirs is defined, by their treatment towards me.

Their actions may dim,
Their light from within,
But I can keep mine forever aglow.

What we say and what we do,
Is only ours to own.

We must live with the consequences.
The good, the bad, even our *inactions* last.

So, with clarity and caution, choose.
The words and actions you use.

Not letting another's poor state of mind,
In any way influence how you, define YOU.

Just put on your big-girl pants and DO what you've got to do. Keeping kindness and love in focus while you live by that golden rule.

In turn maybe someday, others will catch on and choose to live that rule too.

Kindness

Let's all take down our defenses and allow ourselves to be infected with a new virus.

Let's use an almost obsolete word to name it -

Kindness

Let's, *come in-contact with,* as many people as we can, hopefully to infect them as well.

This new virus is easily contracted with just a gentle human touch, words spoken to lift somebody up, a simple little smile, and friendly wave of the hand.

Watch the virus spread like wildfire across the land.

There should never be a search for a cure.

For inevitably, it's without the virus we will certainly all die.

Let's develop our new world order.

Let our NEW "new norm" be

Just simply to be

KIND.

Good Vibrations

Let's try an experiment:
Everyone just focus your thoughts on good.
Everyone focus your thoughts on what you want your life and the world to be.
Do this every waking hour instead of watching the media on TV.
Instead of arguing about which political party is right.
Concentrate all your thoughts on the opposite of all that, every day and every night.
Changing the energies you take within; will change the energies you send out.
Perhaps if everyone did this -
Real change would come about...

Kinder-Garden

If we can learn but ONE WORD, we shall soar...
We are put on this earth to learn and grow.

Sometimes during our process of learning, of growing, people are hurt, we *are* hurt, often hurting ourselves.

It's most often that the hurting we do to others stems from hurts we ourselves have experienced.

It seems like a viscous cycle with no purpose.

But because the One who created us for a purpose allows the hurt to happen, we can trust (though difficult), that there is a reason for everything and as it is said - everything has its season.

The most authentic and unconditional love grows from the most painful of hurt and suffering.

We know this to be true by being a spiritual witness to what Christ endured for us on the cross.

He *still* endures for us if we allow him to do so.

If we open our hearts to receive His undying love and if we open our minds to believe what our eyes can't see but our hearts can feel.

It is then we too can endure whatever hurt comes our way and we are able to forgive the hurts that have come to us and forgive ourselves for the hurts we have caused others, *and ourselves*.

God is the WORD
And Love is A word
And both are ONE in the same

Be the Bulldozer Not the Ground

Until you stop seeing yourself as "victim" you'll never get anywhere in life. So, stop beating yourself down.

We all have our share of baggage we carry. Some, no doubt are burdened with heavier loads than others. But it's important to remember that you are not alone.

Everyone has things that happened to them in their lives. Battered feelings from childhood. From adulthood, torn hearts. Many reasons to be scarred. The secret to success is to leave it all in the dust. Bury the pain of those wounds and teach yourself to trust.

Sometimes it helps to reassure ourselves that we didn't (and don't) necessarily have it any worse or better than others. The important thing is to use adversities as fuel to overcome, remembering to be compassionate towards others as well as with us. Though we are all traveling our own unique journeys, our paths are connected in the bigger picture.

Switch your mindset into gear. Move yourself forward and plow past those old life hurdles. Get a grip on the baton. Tuck away those worn-out patterns of fear. Get over it and just move on. Issues that once paralyzed you, can be transformed into the motivation that sets you free. The secret is that only YOU lock the doors *and* hold the keys.

All the lies that leave us blind, from viewing the world from colorful minds. The so-called truths that teach us wrong from right, blur our imaginations, to see ourselves only in black and white. Limits put upon us that distort our reality, extinguishing our bright to be the light we were created to be.

Let those things that served to bind, be the springboards into a new-found life. Release them once and for all. Leap beyond your wildest dreams and don't be afraid to fall. You will always land on your feet in the place you were destined to be.

Stop letting your future be a playground for your past to prey. Stop allowing fear to devour your dreams, filling you with regret.

Begin today to be authentic YOU. It's what you were destined to do.

Gratitude

Take a trip through Gratitude, whenever trials befall you.

Trials and tribulations do not discriminate. We all go through them, and they usually come when we are the least ready to handle them. When bad things happen our first reaction is not always the best. Sometimes we don't wait before we react. If we can condition ourselves to stop and look at the situation through a lens of gratitude rather than attitude, we will be able to respond, rather than react. We will be able to use the unfortunate to embrace the fortunate.

I believe that everything happens for a reason. And with everything that happens in our lives we are given an opportunity. When it's an uninvited occurrence we can use it as a chance to grow. We can use it as a learning experience. A chance to discover things about ourselves (some of which we may be unwilling to see). And of course, when good fortune falls into our universe, we can take the time to appreciate, praise and give thanks for it and more importantly NEVER take it for granted.

With anything you are going through if approached with a mindset of gratitude, you will pass through the trial with much more ease. Just by incorporating a few short words in your day like Bless You, Thank You, Excuse Me, and Please.

We can get through anything life throws in our way when our attitude is aligned with GRATITUDE.

EPA of the Mind

Polluting the mind, or rather *not*.

From the Daily Stoic by Ryan Holiday, today's lesson spoke to my heart because I am all too familiar with how polluting one's mind, especially one's *own* mind can inhibit your ability to breathe. It talked about the functions of the mind and how ultimately our goal is to not allow it to be polluted.

One way I am finding to keep the pollution levels of my own mind at a functioning level is to be more accepting of my own faults and tendencies. By refraining from the usual berating of myself about not living up to my imagined *perfect* standards, but rather to continue to strive to realign my thoughts and actions. Not to make perfectly straight, as I tend to want to do (I believe a perfectionist's, desire, or NEED to be perfect IS pollution to the mind, body, and soul), but merely to align to ensure a more *balanced* state of mind, body, and soul.

It's that black or white, all or nothing mindset that causes the toxic levels of mind pollution to suffocate a soul. I'm learning to heed my inner warning system.

A positive thought is like fresh air to the mind.

To Be or Not to Be, the person I claim to be

Who am I and What Do I Stand For?

Often the person we feel we are, is not the one we show to others. For instance, I would say that I am a very caring individual. I feel deeply for those who are going through hardship and turmoil. I claim to believe in various organizations that strive to help these individuals. But those are only feelings and words. What have I really DONE for these I say I care about? I claim to be a giving person, but do I really give as I should, or do I just feel like I want to give, but don't do it? I have always had a strong desire to do something positive and really make a difference. But I seem to have always had a good reason (excuse) not to. So, when will the day come when I put my GOOD INTENTIONS to work.

That is one of the ways I am trying to change, or I should say better myself in this new year. To DO some things that will make a difference in people's lives. Not just feel for them. To be the person I desire to be and to stop being *lazy* about it. To stop putting off until tomorrow those things that would serve as a great blessing today for someone in need.

Talk is cheap and good intentions are just that, intentions. But ACTIONS are what make the world go around.

4
VIP's
(very important people, places, and pets)

I Saw You Today

Mom, I saw you today.
Getting ready for work,
Tidying up my clothes,
Splashing water on my face.
Walking past my full-length mirror
There you were.
Your reflection couldn't have been any clearer.

Mom, I saw you today.
Above the many pots, pans, and dishes,
Under the clear wet splash.
It couldn't have been any clearer,
You were there,
I saw your hands.

The day was long, and the pain was aflare,
My feet throbbed with ache.
My back and hips felt like any movement would cause a break.
Mom, I saw you today.

You were there, and I knew,
You lived that pain, too.

Your essence reflects upon me, Mom,
And as I grow older,
with each passing day,
I see you more and more.

I am now a reflection of you.
My hands depict toil as yours did, too.
My face, with every wrinkle and crease,
more and more resembles yours.
My bones and muscles ache,
As yours did every day.

And even though you're gone
Mom, I saw you today.

I can only hope that my heart
Reflects at least a glimpse of what yours was
And that someday, my reflection
Would grace the hearts
of those that I have loved

Warning – I'm Gonna Use the F-Word

FAT

I had to get fat to learn to love myself

Sad to say but I had to get thicker skin to truly see and appreciate the woman within

Women who struggle with this will probably agree

Wearing oversized clothes to hide

Really only fosters the hideous lie

That we are somehow less because we weigh more

That we should care what others think

Or that we should feel we must shrink

To truly fit in

NO

LADIES

OF EVERY SIZE

Stop feeding those lies

Love, accept, and appreciate the woman you are

Without the adjectives which imply

You need to be of a certain size

Let's all grow together

In being kinder to ourselves

Because as it relates to love

One size, fits all

Thoughts at Sunrise

If I didn't have a family

A job

Responsibilities day to day

Would I choose while in my bed

To simply stay

Without a force to motivate the actions I should take

Would my life just simply be

Hours spent

Without intent

Minutes ticking by

Every day a repeat of time

And would this space

be the place

I would choose to remain

If I didn't have a family

A job

Responsibilities day to day

It would seem a life's mundane

Is the thread to keep one sane

For without it

In my bed

I would remain

Dragonflies, Deer, and a Hummingbird

A couple of years ago my sister-in-law called to say my brother was going out to the cemetery to pay our parents a visit, and he was wondering if I would want to tag along. My first thought was NO because I was dead tired and my feet (as usual) were killing me, but with a quick second thought I said sure I would go along. I can't remember if it was a holiday visit (Memorial Day or Father's Day perhaps) - my memory fails, however the memory of that day and that visit to the cemetery will never fade.

I mentioned to my brother that my initial response was going to be no but then I thought what the heck I haven't been there in a while and besides I can chat with mom about these feet. My poor mother had foot pain too and now I know first-hand, how she must have felt.

I also wanted to ask for their prayers for some personal stuff going on, so although I was apprehensive because of my physical fatigue, pain, and the inclement weather situation (storm / tornado warnings were reported), I decided that going was a good idea.

We arrived at the cemetery, and it looked like rain. It had been raining for literally days so no surprise would it have been if it did rain. I mentioned it to my brother but got no response.

We said our hellos to those buried at the site, mom, dad, our uncle and aunt. We couldn't have been there more than a couple of minutes when this dragonfly began to flutter all around me. It simply would not stop. No matter which way I moved it just kept buzzing past my face and all around me. I tried sitting on the stone bench my uncle had purchased for the spot when my aunt passed. It was situated just beside and under the branches of a tree that adorned the backside of the cemetery. The branches did not deter the little dragonfly from buzzing around my body. It was the darndest thing and neither me nor my brother could get over the fact that this insect could not seem to leave me be. Soon, another one joined in, or so it seemed, although it was difficult to even look straight ahead with all the darting back and forth that was going on. Now there were two dragonflies causing quite the frenzy.

My brother and I both commented repeatedly on the fact that these dragonflies would simply not stop flying all about. And they only flew around me. They left my brother alone. Finally, after several minutes of this - they were suddenly, just gone.

No sooner did we notice they departed when I see in the woods directly behind us, a deer. Naturally I started snapping photos. I told my brother to look and then I saw another. There were two and they stayed there staring at me as I attempted to digitally snap the best possible shot.

After a few minutes they too departed.

I looked up at the sky and it did look like a storm was coming. There were warnings out and as usual I was having a bit of anxiety. I just wanted to get home before the storm hit. My brother on the other hand doesn't let things such as the weather or anything out of his control worry him. And he pointed that fact out to me in his usual (annoyed with my fear) way.

We left and I don't think a storm ever did hit.

Later that evening I was sitting on a chair in our living room, peering out at the outside and suddenly right in front of the door a hummingbird came and just hovered, fluttering right in front of the glass door.

I frantically tried to capture its wonder on my digital device, and I couldn't help but think this was more than just a coincidence that I would be visited by first the dragonflies, then the deer and now this beautiful hummingbird.

There have been many things going on that I have had no control over. Loved one's lives dangling by threads, lots of worry filling my head. Lots of pain, sadness, uncertainty. All the things I would have sat with my mom to discuss. She always knew when I was hurting both emotionally and physically and she could always relate because she had lived the same kind of aches and pains, and she too underwent many of life's normal challenges. Dad was much more silent, but you knew he'd be there to lend a strong arm when your life seemed beyond repair.

So, I knew as I witnessed those beautiful visitors, they came as a reminder, that we're never alone.

By the fluttering of a dragonfly, a nod from some deer, and the glinting of a hummingbird, I was comforted. This big world is full of wonderment. Could the Creator of the universe send forth creatures from nature to remind me that I am not alone? And to reassure me that my loved ones are especially always near, and maybe they even send us signals in the form of dragonflies, or deer.

Perhaps by the sight of a hovering hummingbird we can resist the need to worry and relax in the knowledge that, we have what it takes to weather any storm that should come our way.

Body Armor

Our body is in essence, an armor,

That protects our precious soul.

And by its very appearance,

A warrior's life is told.

For whatever the soul has endured,

The *body* wears its scars.

Added weight protects,

The hurt the soul has felt.

Lines and wrinkles upon the face,

Show the hands a soul was dealt.

A life of joy shows with upward curves,

And its pains are the lines facing down.

A soul's story is told from its body,

From the top of one's head to the tips of one's toes.

Chronic pain in its parts caused from heartaches suffered within.

For our hearts are only protected, by the thinnest layers of skin.

Many hearts are worn for all the world to see.

Those are the souls who suffer the most, for their vulnerability.

A thinner body may portray one whose soul is ill.

And often a sickly soul - cannot be saved by any man-made pills.

Only by grace and belief in the powers of the soul's mind,

Can one's body become healed and whole, with patience, over time.

Our bodies are the armor that protects our precious soul.

The appearance of which,

A warrior's story is told.

He Wants You to Know

He gave you strong shoulders to carry burdens

He wants you to know

It's ok to set down your load

He gave you a big heart to feel other's pain

He wants you to know

When yours is crushed

His love will ease the ache

He gave you a yearning and a voice to be heard

He wants you to know

Always seek His truth first

He will give you His Word

To shepherd His herd

And when you grow weary

He wants you to know

The narrower the road

The heavier the load

But it's the path by which He leads

He wants you to know

It's ok

To lay your burdens at His feet

Trust Him to carry you

During times when standing proves too tough

He wants you to know

He knows every challenge that you'll face

Lean on Him

He will be your brace

His love will never fade

He wants you to know

Tip Your Hat to a Woman

As a fellow woman, I am not alone

In my wardrobe of many hats

My head must adorn

Sometimes they may not fit too well

But despite too big or too small

Their responsibilities

On MY shoulders always fall

Many women can dutifully say

They are the main *bread makers*

And in more ways than one

Unlike back in the day

Today roles are different, that a woman must play

Many jobs of varying skills

Of which a few I'll name

From keeping the household on budget

To checking temps to doling out pills

Investment brokers some are

Yet some are not

But a woman's pencil either way

Proves just as sharp

As is her keen eye

YOUR GROUNDED is ringing in the kiddo's ears

Before their lips even begin to mouth the lie

From veterinarian to all the pets

To the neighborhood cookie jar

The many hats a woman must wear

Her to do list stretches far

But with beauty and grace

she adorns every, one

Sometimes simultaneously

For a woman's work is rarely done

Her hands are always busy

Her feet though aching they run

Overflowing from head to toe

Is her heart brimming with love.

So, tip your hat to a woman

because

The woman who wears many hats

Leaves behind some pretty big shoes to fill

My Shadow

My thought on Monday November 1st, 2021, was...

Today I lost my shadow. My pillow pal. Today we lost our pet cat Tuppie.

We got Tuppie along with her twin sister back in 2009. They were a gift from me to two of my daughters. They were both in a play The King and I, put on by our local drama guild at our local theatre. We had just lost our community cat Marbles while they were doing the play. The girls were in elementary school and the play (during the summer) was very time consuming. They were both real troopers about doing it, well most of the time. I did get some flack.

I refer to Marbles as our community cat because she originally belonged to our neighbors. But too many a night Marbles was left out because the owners worked crazy hours, so I began letting her in our garage and feeding her (I let the neighbors know of course and they were fine with it). Well in 2008 when I went back to work, I became the owner with the crazy hours and my mom (who lived right next door), began doing the same thing. Letting Marbles in her house and feeding her.

Marbles suddenly passed while the girls were doing the play, so I decided to get them each a kitten as a reward. It was a surprise, and I picked the names after a couple characters from the play, Tuppie (after the character Tup Tim) and Ana (after the character Ana). Of course, if the girls wanted to, they could have picked different names, but they didn't.

Tuppie developed cancer a few years ago. She had two lumps removed, at separate times but the cancer was already too far gone and so we were told she would probably develop more lumps, which she did. There wasn't anything to do in terms of surgery, it would be too extensive, and she probably wouldn't survive so we let her be. Her lumps grew and new ones formed, but Tuppie remained the active, happy little kitty she always was. Even though technically she was my daughter's cat, Tuppie ended up being my little buddy. Everywhere I was, Tuppie was. Right behind my head when I was sitting on the sofa. Atop the desk while I was doing dishes, or cooking in the kitchen. Sitting atop the bathroom scale at bedtime when I went in to change and get ready for bed. And of course, curled up atop my pillow or beside me in bed.

For the last couple of weeks, I had been camping out in the living room as Tuppie's largest tumor began bleeding and we had to keep it wrapped. It developed an infection, so we asked the vet for some medication to give her along with the pain medicine. The first round worked but not too long after, I could tell the infection was not gone as she developed an odor. I did get more medicine, but it just wasn't clearing up the odor, so I knew the infection was too far gone and by then the tumor was bleeding again too.

Tuppie was still having good days. She was eating well, drinking water and using the potty. She was still purring but by the end of that last week, although she was still eating, drinking, going potty, she was not looking like herself. I wasn't noticing her purring and she just looked unhappy, so I made the call.

We all wanted Tuppie to go when it was her time. We all felt that if she was having good days, eating, drinking, going potty, getting around, purring, and enjoying being around us, not seeming to be in pain - we didn't want to take matters into our own hands. We wanted her to go when the good Lord took her and not before.

We loved her. I loved her. She was the sweetest cat there ever was. Life without Tuppie seemed like - NO, we just couldn't. But when Tuppie started looking at me like she was, I knew that we couldn't keep her just because we couldn't let her go. We couldn't let her go on with this tumor that was now worse and with no sign of ever getting better. We couldn't be cruel. Tuppie deserved much more than that. So, I made the call.

We took her to the vet for the shot that would give her the peace and rest that she deserved.

Hard is an understatement.

Sad doesn't even begin to describe how I felt and still feel.

Let the mourning begin. I couldn't be more devastated if a family member had passed. Well ok yes of course I put my family as a higher priority and they have a more intimate and genuine love, but still, we value our pets nearly as much as we value our family (human) members. They are part of our family and losing one hurts just as much.

I'm certain I am not alone in this reality. Think of how much time you spend with your pet. They are there for you during all of life's woes. They are right beside you when you are sad and crying, they are there licking and purring and rubbing their cute little furry faces up against yours as if to say, *it's ok, I'm here,*

I love you unconditionally, and they do. They do love us and give us their utmost attention and time.

So yes, I, even more than my daughter or any other family member, I am mourning the loss of Tuppie our cat. I am hurting and I miss her terribly. She was the sweetest little cat there ever was.

My only consolation is the certainty in my heart that she is at rest, at peace, in no pain, and purring happily ever after over the rainbow.

Spectacular

That's it.

There are no big spectacular moments...

It's just a million little ordinary ones that when bound together - is spectacular.

The most ordinary of lives are the most spectacular.

It's all in the way we choose to view those little ordinary moments.

Savor each one.

Enjoy every second, every *morsel* of your life - ENJOY.

There are no coincidences, everything happens for a reason. Be open to this realism and you will notice the hand of God meticulously guiding. Every life is part of an orchestra and a masterpiece of our Heavenly Father, *Artist* of all that is, ever has been, and ever will be. He is a constant in your life, in my life, in *every* life - everything living. And it is simply magnificent.

Whether a believer or not, He is still the great and loving director of the most beautiful orchestra of all - LIFE. Everyone has their own unique note to play. Each note having a distinct sound, tone, vibration which brings its own characteristic to life's symphony. Each of us is an instrument and every single instrument, every single life plays an integral part to the whole.

Living life in awe keeps us humble, never taking for granted this beautiful gift of life.

This magical, miraculous ensemble we are each a part of.

Every moment is an opportunity to cherish - whatever is happening - moment to moment, live in it fully. Relish in its beauty. Relish in the beauty of it all.

Just keep moving forward.

Living every ordinary moment.

And when your journey nears its end, you'll look back at the big picture and it will be SPECTACULAR.

Be Comfortable in Your Cabin

It may be crazy out in the world today

But on my little part of the planet all is well

We are safe

We are sound

We are under roof

We are above the ground

We have food - yes plenty

Our pockets jingle some

But most of all

We still have Love

Mismatched

Patterns. They say you can cross patterns as long as the colors match. Not so with the Hawaiian pattern, as was proven when my husband walked out of the bedroom.

We were getting ready for my daughter's recital, oh how I wish I had a camera shot of *my* expression when I saw *him* walk out in a pair of cargo shorts, black with a lime green Hawaiian print on them and a blue, pastel, button down shirt, also with a Hawaiian print on it, but a brightly multicolored one. Clearly the color scheme wasn't the only mismatching going on. Shorts with a button-down shirt wasn't making it either.

Well, the phrase badly dressed tourist was an understatement.

It got me to thinking that some things no matter how hard you try or how badly you want them, just aren't meant to be put together.

This rule does not only apply to fashion, but some people are also just too mismatched to ever happily cohabit. When separated they can be functional, blending perfectly within the surroundings that suit them best. But when together, it can be an explosive blend of - opposite.

Let's take a closer look at those Hawaiian shorts, which would work perfectly with a shirt with just the right shade of green in it to bring out that element in the fabric of the shorts. Though subtle with the right pairing can make otherwise boring attire really pop.

And this is surely true of the brightly patterned button-down shirt - it too, with a better type of trouser could be a perfect match.

The two together may not be a match, but simply by choosing another pattern to pair them with, the separate patterns can complement each other.

But sometimes you just must work with what you've got. Simply picking and choosing just won't do.

Like in marriage, you're stuck with me, and I'm stuck with you. So, you learn to compromise. Adjust wherever and whenever adjustments are needed, to achieve the best possible outcome for both to be their best.

Hmmm sometimes I wonder whom is the patterned, button-down-shirt and who is the patterned trousers in our relationship because clearly, we are not always the best matched but if each is willing to make some minor adjustments most common relationship wrinkles can be ironed out. Focusing on making a change on the *inside* can alter the way the other views them from the *outside*. With each adjusting their normal patterns even slightly, can make two opposites - a perfect match.

Behold

If beauty is in the eye of the beholder, isn't it about time you opened your eyes to behold?

Be happy in the skin you are in. Your beauty is not only skin deep...

We waste so much time, money, and energy in trying to BE different, LOOK different, and FEEL different.

Imagine how you might *glow* if you simply accepted that you're beautiful just the way you are, no make-up required. The word itself isn't real - make-up - the result is *made up*.

Imagine how you might *thrive* if you accepted yourself for the person, you are, strengths and faults alike without trying to adjust your personality to what your mind has convinced you, you *should* be.

What an incredible sense of freedom we could achieve if we allowed ourselves, just to *be*.

And what if instead of buying and trying fads of remedies to feel great, you simply began a new *routine* to start your day?

Try inhaling deep breaths and long exhales without the added sighs. Try waking every morning grateful simply to be *alive*. Try making some time for nature. Try exercising too. Try nurturing your body by feeding it healthy foods.

Watch your soul become energized and your mood will lift too.

With an everyday like this, how could you feel anything BUT good!

Be happy in the skin you are in.

Behold the beauty that is *YOU*.

Best Friend

Loss of someone you love is devastating and probably one of the most difficult emotional challenges we are faced with and forced to survive. But losing a pet has its own unique emotions. Its own depth of sadness and loss.

I think it is because pets love completely unconditionally. No matter what type of person you are, kind, loving, or a pain in the butt, your pet thinks you're the greatest person that ever walked the face of the earth. Your pet will wait for you to come home, for as many hours as it takes - they will wait. Pets rarely, if ever get mad at their *best friend*. I don't even think they are capable of that.

Pets are miraculously intuitive of their owner's state of mind and heart. They will be by your side to give a loving lick for every tear you cry.

Any loss is difficult. But the loss of a pet carries a unique sense of grief. They are the furry friends who are always there for every heartbreak of your life.

Our loving pet was a long-haired miniature Dachshund named, *Crystalbell*. We were blessed to have her with us for the last twelve and a half years of her life. We got her when she was just two years old. She bonded immediately with the whole family, but she and I had a special bond.

She was the best, floppy eared, furry, true blue *best friend* to us all.

No matter how busy my day was spent, her big brown eyes were on me and her ear was slightly bent, waiting for any form of a greeting from me, and a kiss upon her head. She was at my side and in my lap for every heartache I've endured. She was my furry friend, and her love was true and pure.

My heart will be warmed, by the many memories of snuggling time we shared. She will forever remain in all our hearts for the rest of our lives.

Any loss is an extremely difficult life experience, but the loss of a pet has a different level of grief with its own sadness and tears.

Know that with this post I am sending hugs to anyone who has lost a pet AKA,

Best Friend.

5
MIDDLE GROUND

Yin, Yang, and Everything In-Between

The Ebb and Flow of Life

I recall some time ago talking to a dear friend and writing mentor whose energy, enthusiasm, and zest for life reminded me that it is ok to have ups and downs and to have our perspectives be continually shifted from one thing to another.

It's just the ebb and flow of living.

The yin, the yang of life.

You must look for the gray.

Between the black and white.

Feel the feelings as they go out and come in.

You will be fine in the long run.

Just do what you can.

Give whatever you can give.

And when faced with a day that you have trouble even removing your body from bed,

Just lie there for a moment, let your mind visit thoughts and memories, good and bad that you find keep dancing around your head.

If feeling blue, let yourself *feel* every shade.

Let sadness drip from your emotions like branches of a tree drip heavy from pouring rain.

Let your heart be a sponge to soak up the mess of it all.

When your good and ready, get up and out even if all you can muster is a slow but steady crawl.

Today may not be great,

But tomorrow is only a day away.

So, feel, deal, and wait.

Today may be yin.

Tomorrow may be yang,

It's the ebb and flow of living, just the same.

Let Go Your Ego

Be gentle with your ego

It knows not what it does

Allow your spirit to protect it

by embracing it in love

It only acts out of concern and its desperate need for control

It's been tricked to think it can

Little does it know

The heart is where your rudder lies

It will steer you as you go

Be gentle with your ego

It thinks but doesn't know

Snack Break

Implementing little habits throughput your day increases productivity by improving mood, spirit, and overall health and well-being.

The Fruit Salad

The other day I took fruit to work for my snack. That's not unusual, I take fruit to work every day. But this day I had the brilliant idea to spruce it up a bit and cut all the fruit up and toss it all in a bowl to have a fruit salad rather than just, an apple, grapes, and a banana. I tossed everything into a brown paper lunch sack and off I went. (I have a paring knife and bowl at work).

Now this day, like any other day at the office, was its usual - busy.

Before I knew it, I was already in starving mode and reached in the brown paper sack for the banana, deciding that I didn't have time to cut the fruit up so I would just eat it whole like I normally do.

Then I remembered the pact I had made (to myself), to start implementing little habits throughout my day to increase my productivity by improving my mood, spirit, and overall health and well-being.

So, for once I decided to take my own advice by following through with my plan to take care of myself.

So, I cut the apple, sliced the banana, and sprinkled the grapes on top, voila` - a tossed salad.

Wow did the snack take on a whole new vibe. A fresh new sensation. Like a party in my mouth for my tastebuds.

I took the time to enjoy my snack - not just rush through while doing my work. No, I actually took a snack *break*.

What a difference it made to the rest of my day.

Practice Trolley Riding

Amazingly I feel concretely balanced in body while feeling emotionally and physically out of balance in mind.

I take a stance, feet parallel with big toes touching, readying myself for a quick yogic morning stretch. It is a practice I love yet of late have gotten way out of sync with. I rarely take the time even though on the sporadic days that I do, I realize just how therapeutic it is for both my body and mind.

After a quick stretch, I look to see if Joyce Meyer Ministries is on the television. I love to listen to her messages and just like the stretching practice, listening daily use to be a part of my daily routine. I begin to enter the channel number on the remote going from memory (almost always a mistake). I enter the number 564. My usual starting point as I know the spiritual channels on our plan are somewhere in the 500-channel range.

I press 460 by mistake (Dyslexia kicks in) and lo and behold that channel was the exact channel I needed. There she was, just beginning her message. And boy did I need to hear the message. It was exactly in line with what was troubling me.

Some call these happenings coincidence.

But those who believe in a higher power call them God-incidences.

It can also be called (taking from the profound teaching of Dr Wayne Dyer) -
"Grabbing the straps and riding the trolley. Letting life unfold."

And sometimes on the days we may not be strong enough to grab the straps, the trolley grabs hold of us to see that we don't miss our ride.

Normalcy

I'm done with it!

I am ready for some non-normalcy.

Since our normal has now become - well, what it has become, with this COVID, I want anything but normalcy in twenty twenty-one.

I would like a new - norm.

Unlike the last new-norm this one shall be full of LIFE, living, laughing, loving, loveliness, lockdown-less, lots of good, lots of hope, prosperity, forgiveness, fairness, getting along, unity, real news, or better - no news, respect, consideration, health, well-being, thriving - oh I could go on and on.

But I'll end with *all wishes coming true for me for you - for everyone.* Yes, this shall be the new norm of twenty twenty-one.

Oh, and one more thing

A new word or phrase to replace *new norm*

How about Old Normal Returns or, A Better Normal Blooms, *or...again, I could go on and on.*

Breakfast Groove

At the end of the day, it's not about what a person is doing to you. It's more about what *you* are doing to be the person you want to be.

Don't let another's lack of, be the measure of *your* integrity.

Don't react. And certainly, don't *overreact*.

Just take a moment or two (if needed), to choose *your* best response. And know that in some cases that may be - none.

There is a lot to be said for - NO response.

In the end it's you that you must face in the mirror. And it's your inner voice that will be pecking at your ear with murmurs of regret.

So, stay true to the person *you* want to be.

And know, that may mean to simply - not speak.

A lot can be heard in - *silence*.

Do You See What I See?

Shift your perspective from its usual frame of ME focus

and surround yourself in the view.

Open your eyes to the world as others see it and you may notice it is not always about you.

When you begin to explore with a wider lens a truer picture begins to take shape.

With vision crystal clear, we may finally see on the horizon - a chance for real change.

Self-centered. Self-absorbed. Self-serving. All basically mean the same thing. It's being focused on the inward, which distorts a person's view of the outward.

There is a great big world out there and its spinning does not revolve around YOU.

That doesn't take away from the importance of every single soul. That doesn't mean that every breath you take isn't ordained for a greater purpose. I believe it is. I believe we are all here for a very specific reason. We *all* have purpose. We *all* are important. We *all* are constantly in the focus of His (our Higher Power's) loving eyes. We are ALL part of the bigger picture.

But it's our lives pieced together with love and compassion that makes the picture ART. It's our capacity to weave forgiveness and acceptance within our lives that keep the tapestry from falling apart. It's only by embracing the needs of others, that our own can be met.

So, *all* - TOGETHER *now!* - Is where we *need* to get.

Time is running out. We *all* must act now. We are going to lose the shot when darkness blurs the light, if we don't bring out the wider lens and retire our narrow-minded I's.

We have a new year approaching. Let's open our hearts to a broader view. Focus a little less on the ME and a little more on the YOU. Perhaps a brighter world will come into *our* view.

Transitions

Life is full of them.

Literally.

Life is *transition*.

From the very beginning of everything. Every form of plant, animal, human. From one point moving on to the next.

Earth. *Everything*, in the universe is...

Transition.

On our life journey we go through layers and layers of transitions both physically and emotionally every day.

My entire family (me included) has been going through several life-changing transitions for the past few years now, most of which have not been pleasant in any way shape or form. In fact, it has been a challenge at times to even transition from one day to the next, but we do because we're resilient.

But alongside the difficult there are also good transitions that we experience. Watching are children from pregnancy to birth, from infant to toddler, from one school year to the next and all the years leading up to and including adulthood. Our own lives transitioning all at the same time. Many of us are or will soon be empty nesters. So again, we are out in a place of change. We have the choice of whether we will become stagnant or grow with all the new available possibilities life now holds.

For me that is what my art has been. A constant, *though slow moving*, transition. With each year opening more doors, to lead me to more possibilities of growth. With the ultimate reward being able to experience the joy of being my individual, creative soul, and sharing that soul with others.

Rethink Your Groove

Sometimes you just need to regroup, take a step back, and rethink *your* groove.

Make the decision that *forward* will be your next move. To step back is to relive the happenings from PAST. Choose to move on from the heartache of all that. What good can come anyway, from looking back, stepping into footsteps that once led you straight into attack?

That pain has already been suffered, and the wounded will be forever scarred. But wounds, if treated can mend, when hardened hearts show mercy, they become pliable enough to bend.

There is nothing one can do with another's choice to hold onto hurt, never allowing the rawness of emotions to lose its burn. Not every memory is a fond one, too often those are few, but we can control which ones hold our focus and which ones we allow to blur.

And though the mind may never completely forget, and a broken heart may always suffer a dull ache, we all can heal but the capacity to forgive is a *choice* that we must make.

You cannot always convince another that *forward* should be their next move. You can only control the direction of your own groove.

Limitless

Too often our lives get stuck in a vacuum. We shift through our life feeling as if we are trying to navigate through a dense fog. We are trapped in a mindset that our personal world is made up of only what we see in our present situation. Like a dream we can see a door *out* of our limiting mindset, yet we don't realize that it can never be opened until WE reach out, grab the handle and turn.

We buy into a belief system that has programmed us, *since practically our birth*, to believe that certain advantages, certain destinies are only possible for the *others*. You know that imaginary elite group of individuals that live and thrive far beyond the lowly ones, *like us*. And so, we just continue to allow all the possibilities of the universe to remain out of *our* grasp.

Open the door where there is no fog. Where the possibilities are endless, as far as our imaginations can see, and then even further beyond that, to the point of where we couldn't even have imagined - where limits are abandoned and LIMITLESS is born.

All we must do - is open the doors.

A Fork in the Road

Of late I feel like I have been on a crash course to my own destruction. I keep making choices which I know are not in my best interest. Eating foods, I know will only add to my weight, while depleting my energy, staying up too late trying to accomplish the things that could have been accomplished earlier had I not fallen into one of the many "time suckers" our fast-paced lives are met with daily. And last but not least, emotionally berating myself for doing the previous two.

I took a good look into my inner mirror and seen myself standing at a fork in the gravel road of my life. I say gravel because life has always proved a bit bumpy, though I am grateful for every single bump along the way. The scenario was quite visible in my mind's eye. As was the realization that a choice needed to be made, and it would be mine alone to make.

So, I had a much-needed conversation with me, myself, and I to decide which route I should take. And the conversation went like this...

The first way seems simple it's the one you *too well* know. Continue to move straight ahead on the same old dead-end road. It seems you have been on it your whole life long; it goes on forever but leads to nowhere that you really want to be.

So, you ponder a little longer looking closer at choice two and three.

You could take a chance and veer to the right, the path seems steep but shorter all in all and every sign points to, *this is the way to go.* But you fear traveling on it will only cause your progress to further slow and the burdens will be heavy, from experience this you know, when you realize this is a path you have traveled before.

There is the way to the left, you have never ventured beyond the door. You can see in the distance the path looks quite long but the hardships though many, will seem light, because you'll know the choice, for *you* was right.

Making the decision to change your direction is the first step in changing a stagnant life. If while on your journey you find yourself met with a challenge to make a life changing choice, give yourself a moment to ponder which way you should go when you find yourself at a fork on your own gravel road.

Stop Living a Rerun

Don't live life in a rerun. Hiatus would be a better way to go, or better yet, take a chance and pilot a *new show*.

Making the same mistakes repeatedly is insane. Yet blindly we begin a new day doing, as if on auto pilot, the same things that led us to frustrations the day before.

It's like constantly playing reruns of your life repeatedly. Yes, there's a sense of comfort with its familiarity and yes there is an element of nostalgia, but inevitably what put us in a place of crying ourselves to sleep before, is sure to come up *in the next act*, as it has repeatedly done before.

Yet we continue making the same mistakes, keeping us chained to self-sabotaging habits leading us into failure and restricting us from ever moving forward.

Switch off the internal network of negativity. Stop the constant buzz of critical self-talk. Begin a channel for positive habits to form. Take your life on a new path, see how much better life can play out.

Enjoy your work, leave room to play. Try to experience a new scene every single day. Take *your show* on the road to exhilarating locations. Awake each day with joy and anticipation.

Switch your gear out of couch potato mode. Get up, go out and *create* in your sphere of the world, a new day, and be the star of *your show*.

Breathe

I can't be happy unless -
I won't be satisfied until -
As soon as I -

How many of us tackle the topic of our joy by beginning our day muttering these words?

Or at the very least with those very words ringing in our minds?

STOP!

The time for happiness is right this very moment. Joy is found in the NOW.

I have heard the wisdom (author unknown), *grow a backbone in place of that wishbone girl*. No truer words have been spoken.

Embrace what you've got.
Let go of wanting what's not.

Waiting for your world to lineup perfectly will take more time than your entire lifetime. In fact, it will never happen. But what will happen is your lifetime will end.

And just as the end nears, you'll no doubt be muttering words that have this ring to them... *I wish I had not wasted so much of my life waiting for everything to be just right.* You'll realize it *was* just right; in the moment you were waiting for it to be.

Every moment is lined up perfectly -
If you still breathe

Calm Indifference

A Series of ANWERS

In the spirit of taking a more active role in my own peace of mind and creating within myself and my surroundings a sense of calm, I have embarked on a journey of learning to be more indifferent about the things that really don't matter. Below are my answers to a few questions that touch on having an *attitude of indifference*.

I don't, except perhaps to lend some moral support, help build a person up rather than join in trapping them down...*Why do I need to care that someone else screwed up?*

By realizing, their unimportance and accepting my lack of control...*How can I cultivate indifference to unimportant things?*

I would no doubt regret far less...*What would happen if I took a second to cool down?*

Pretty often. People seem to believe that I know what I'm doing, while *I* generally *question* my every move...*How often do I question the things others take for granted?*

If you're asking me, the answer is YES. If you're asking others, the answer is NO... *Do I see and assess myself accurately?*

I am trying diligently to stand with the philosophers most days but find myself hopelessly in the snare of the mob, a lot...*Am I standing with the philosopher or the mob?*

All of them...*How many of my limitations are self-imposed?*

Taking stock in yourself and what is best for your own peace is a way of thinking and living that I certainly aspire to. It is difficult but by learning to cultivate an attitude of indifference for the unimportant factors that fill up our time - we can spend more time cultivating the precious commodity of - *our own peace.*

What's Your Point?

I don't think *my* point of view can be seen through *your* narrow mind.

I have long suspected that a family member was slightly leaning in terms of political views.

It seemed that when surfing news channels and an opposing view became audible the channel was promptly changed.

Well, being the (I like to think) fair-minded person that I am, I freely gave that person the benefit of the doubt and concluded it was just my imagination.

But recently another family member pointed the exact same thing out. I guess my imagination was spot on.

I have never been prone to lean one way or another. I like to take a broader view. And besides that, I spend very little time viewing period. I would much rather spend my free time reading, writing, and meditating in my own little bubble with earbuds tucked in listening to and being in my own *Yoga Zone*.

Other family members thrive in the chaotic antics of the politicians' turned celebrities on the local news (AKA gossip) shows.

When I saw that I was not the only one that was awakened to an obvious tendency, it gave me a reason, to ponder. That kind of behavior, though I'm sure nothing new, could be the reason this epidemic has ensued.

By epidemic I mean the media, political NONSENSE we are all bombarded with. Just mention a political point of view and a once just minded human quickly turns into a rabid animal ready to attack, unless of course, your *viewpoints* are in the same direction as theirs.

No one wants to even take the time to hear what is being said by the other side. How can any problem be rectified? When mindsets choose to be deaf? They all just talk, and mostly yell, not hearing anything else being said. How can we expect to move forward when our leaders choose the path to a dead end?

If all this narrow mindedness, has trickled down to the viewer, the ones that cast the vote, my view is growing smaller where there use to be a sliver of hope.

The only way for us *middle ground* leaners to survive the surmounting madness is to patiently sit in our bubble, earbuds safely tucked in, listening to and staying in our own little Yoga Zone of gladness.

Plans? Don't Plan on Them

It's all about time management, they say. But I keep running out of time to manage.

There just doesn't seem to be enough hours in the day to accomplish all that I have set out to do.

The problem is my caboose keeps jumping from one track to another. So, I never actually reach any of my destinations. No project ever gets completely done.

When one feels they have *too* much to do staying on one task at a time proves difficult. Even small tasks become overwhelming and when *everything* feels overwhelming, *nothing* gets done.

Time Management is important. But when your life is in a state of - *overwhelm*, following a time management plan is impossible. Your daily responsibilities must actually *be* manageable.

The word *delegation* comes to mind and so I pose a question to myself, "are there other family members that could take the load off of my shoulders?" The answer is YES. But it is up to me to *ask* for help. It is up to me to *assign* the chores. I would bet that I am not alone in this. How many others experience this as well? Pose the same question. You too will get the same answer. ASK for help. ASSIGN the chores. DELEGATE MORE. And if you have the resources, you might consider hiring someone to come in and lend a hand. It may be well worth the cost.

The point is to make whatever changes necessary to lead you to SUCCESS, because if you don't you will continue to end your day, your weekend, your week, month, and every single year after

year after year, feeling like a failure. Normal everyday living, doing the daily things that result in a tidy house, records, and bills kept in order, etc., will continue to be a
challenge. Large *and* small tasks will seem overwhelming.

Set realistic goals. Remember baby steps will get you to where you want to be a lot faster than NO STEPS. Stay committed to what you set out to do. If you notice a basket of laundry on your way to do the dishes don't stop to fold. Let it go for now and just do those dishes. Then tackle the next thing. Keep this pace each day, it will help you not only get things done but will make you feel so much better. And by the end of an hour, a day, a week, and year after year you will see the difference. Your home, your work, your self-image, your whole life will improve.

This may sound simple, and insignificant to some, but for those who struggle with this daily, it is a huge issue. It's like dragging a gigantic ball and chain around your neck day in and day out. Getting a handle on it is paramount.

Perhaps cliche but true, "No one knows what another person is feeling or understands what they are going through until you have walked in their shoes you haven't got a clue. Show them some understanding and be kind, while they are learning to *manage their time.*

From One's Extreme to Another's

We live in a world of extremes. We've lost the edge of common sense. It's not a recipe for success. It is a poisonous mix. The result is division. And as a society, we have hit a boiling point. Something must give.

We have become politically correct but lost morality. We try children as adults, when often it's the parents who's at fault.

We sentence those with addictions to a life of penalty. But those who rape and murder, with a slap on the hand we set free. None of this makes any sense to me.

There is so much unbalance in our society. Our rulers seem to be leading us towards less unity and more divide. With opinions that collide. Neighbors, strangers, family, friends, used to greet with a smile now turn on each other with vile.

It's a sad state-of-affairs. We've lost the ability to care. With our loss of common sense, mankind's future is hell-bent

We are teetering on the edge of self-destruction. When we create rules to aid in our own extinction.

Oh, we are being led. With lies we're being fed.

And with every swallow of lie a little more we die. As a people with knees bent, we've surrendered to the Culture of Death.

Out of Focus?

Adjust Your Lens

Where has my focus been lately? I ask myself. If the answer is, *on me*, then my next question must be, who has been neglected by my outward focus, directed inward? The answer, everyone.

Often, we get so wrapped up in what is going on in our own lives, we forget about the lives of those closest to us. We lose sight of the simple truth that what is important isn't necessarily what is going on with us. But when we are going through a trying situation, how can we NOT think of how we are being affected? How can we NOT be centered on self, when WE are hurting, depressed, in pain?

The fact is by directing our focus away from ourselves while we are being tested, we begin to feel better. The more attention you put on something, whether it be a pain, hurt feelings, frustration, or depression, the more pronounced those feelings will become. And it is as such when we focus on something or someone else. By putting our attention on others, we can make a pronounced difference in someone's life. And we ultimately feel better ourselves. Without the focus on self, our aches, pains, hurt feelings become smaller.

When we make *ourselves* the smaller point of focus, we can see the bigger picture more clearly.

The In-Between

All the good stuff happens in the middle.

It occurred to me the other day while I was having a quiet reflection of SELF. We tend to focus on the good or the bad. Too often we forget to look at all the *in-between*. We all have strengths and weaknesses to our personalities. It is said that our weaknesses are merely our strengths taken to the extreme. That makes sense, but again what about the *in between*?

And not only the middle ground of our moods and tendencies but our lives in general. All the years, months, days, hours, and minutes we fill up from beginning to end but all the good stuff is how the moments in between are spent.

What about the days we are not doing or being anything but ordinary, mundane, having a nothing kind of day. That to me is the in-between. We don't wake up and set out to do something incredible, we just wake up. We are not particularly happy or sad, just humming along staying in tune with the scene. Those are the sort of days that leave you wide open for surprise. You may meet someone that becomes a lifelong friend. You may have the best day of your life, then tomorrow it could end. You could have the worst luck that anyone's ever known, then tomorrow shows up and changes it all.

The randomness in our lives is what I call the middle. That is the place where the magic happens. Where the memories that last are born.

Think of when you sit down to rock your baby to sleep, you share a special moment, when you first begin to rock. Gazing into each other's eyes in a quiet little spot. Soon her little eyes close with the heaviness of slumber. There. Right, there is where the magic begins for you as a mother. You quietly watch your angel sleep, her little eyelids flutter while having baby dreams. You sit and stare in wonder, thanking your lucky stars. Grateful for the life you have and the one you now hold in your arms. Soon the baby wakes and more moments of joy will be had. But for those precious in-between moments, your heart will forever be glad.

There will be lots and lots of big moments. All sorts of firsts and lasts. But when the nest is empty and you're rocking alone, you'll fondly recall those moments, like when she rode your hip while your shoulder juggled a phone. Those were the times that gave life to your home.

Now back to our own personalities and the many facets of your ME. Embrace and celebrate, the good, the bad, and especially the *in between*.

Shift Your Gears

How are you traveling on your journey? In Park. Drive. Neutral. Or Reverse. Or are you simply STALLED?

You can't move forward if you keep dwelling on regrets. Regrets are part of past disappointments in self or others. Let go and move on. Nothing can change them so don't waste three of your most precious commodities - Breath, Energy, and Time.

Although allowing your mind to remain focused on past regrets can certainly cause unnecessary obstacles to moving forward in your life, there is something to be said for the growth opportunity they hold. I think a healthy balance between taking ownership, (accepting responsibility), and an honest reflection of the behavior that contributed to, then planning for eliminating recurrence, is a good practice to begin. Ultimately letting that regret vanish from our active thoughts and get on with moving ahead.

Don't let your mind keep shifting in reverse, stalling you in the past. Park your attentions there briefly, re-examine any behavior that was a driving force. Curb it and with a neutral mind, move ahead confidently navigating your course.

A Day with a View

I read something that said, "see the world like a poet and an artist." What a delightful thought. How much more love and understanding, compassion and acceptance, if everyone on the planet were to view our world with the eyes of a poet and an artist. How much beauty to observe.

The next thing I read out of my journal entry prompt was "can I find grace and harmony in places others overlook?" My answer...

...On a busy city street, noisy busses stop abruptly, horns honk impatiently at pedestrians passing through red lights before they turn to green, hurriedly they sneak. Flip-flopped feet pause, hunky boots prod, some with children dragging close behind, some smile joyfully at the passers-by. Others simply nod, and some point their noses high, their role is simply, snob.

In all the rush of back and forth, a chaotic scene to some. I see poetic harmony among a city on the run. There is no halt in the rhythm, just a continuous calming buzz of people going about their day, in a city on the run.

They all seem joyful in their own unique way. If not, surely, they would choose to live, in a different sounding day.

This artist paints her picture to occupy her mind. To many, the beauty of the chaos is blind to the eye. But there is grace and harmony, and when you seek, its beauty you will find. The view of the world is different for everyone. I'm grateful for my view today, in a city on the run.

Mind Your Own

If all I control is my mind (my choices, reasoning, and judgment), then why have I wasted so many minutes of precious time worrying about so much that is outside of my control?

The answer: unawareness

We get so accustomed to and comfortable in our thinking habits that we don't even realize that we are being led in a circle. There is no beginning, no end. Just rounding the same turns over again. That is what worry is. It gets us absolutely, nowhere.

Bringing our awareness to what we hold within our reach of control will bounce our old thinking habits right out of that vicious circle of worry.

Over the past weekend, I noticed a marked difference. A shift, if you will, in my usual pattern of mind pacing. It was snowing and my daughter had to leave the house early for an event. Normally I would have offered (her dad), to drive her, worried that she could slip and slide into a predicament. This day, however, I did not feel worried at all. This time, without even thinking about it, I went about my business. I barely even noticed her leaving. I felt completely at ease, and unafraid for her safety out on the possibly slick roads.

Later in the day my other two daughters also had to go out and brave the winter wonderland and again I just simply let them go on their way, remaining focused on what I was involved in. Later that night when my oldest left rather late for a store run - I went to bed confident that she would return safe and sound.

When I laid my head on the pillow, my mind drifted off, and I fell asleep, soundly.

Progress is feeling pretty good. Letting go of old habits and taking a step back from my usual mind pacing and just focusing on what is within my reach of control.

If it's not in my control, I need to let it go. Just MIND MY OWN.

Rock Steady

Steadiness seems to be the topic the latter part of this week not only in my daily reading journal "The Daily Stoic Journal", by Ryan Holiday and Stephan Hanselman, but also in my *actual* personal experience.

Today's journal question "What are sources of unsteadiness in my life?"

Immediately after reading the above question my first instinct was to begin listing the outside elements that cause me to feel unsteady but then realized, again (don't forget this is all a learning experience for me), I am the only one who controls my steadiness or unsteadiness. There are a zillion unsteady factors surrounding me on any given day, some I am painfully aware of because of the proximity, others I am not even aware they exist but still influence the stability I experience or don't. But the only influence good or bad to my steadiness ultimately comes from me. Only *I* control my thoughts, which in turn effect my feelings, which in turn create wellness of body, mind, spirit, or an unhealthy, diseased atmosphere within my vessel. It's all up to me.

Okay, that's all good and well and easy to say, BUT today I was given the gift (I will call it a gift because I do believe that any incident that occurs in our lives will be a springboard for growth or an obstacle to us, depending on how we choose to accept it). Today I chose to accept this incident as an open invitation to grow rather than to fall into the same old pattern I am all too familiar with.

Being drawn into my daughter's knockdown, blow out of an argument over the shared automobile (aka nightmare), via text, it immediately caused my body to react. I found my limbs and chest tightening with the first text message notification that glared on my home screen. Why they find it necessary to include me (when I am miles away from the entire situation both in body and mind), is beyond me. But they always do. Because I am MOM all knowing. Little do they know I cry in the dark feeling like I KNOW NOTHING. But I digress.

The point here is that I had a real-life moment to use what I have been reading about and practicing this week. Not giving anything or anyone other than ME control of my inner peace. *My steadiness.* I am happy to announce that I did it. I went on to have a very enjoyable day. I will also admit that rather than go home after work, when I spotted the nightmare (aka shared automobile) in the driveway, I kept on driving, so I guess that can be viewed one of two ways. *One*, I let the situation control me. Or *two*, I am practicing my time management skills (which I am also trying to improve on). I'll *choose* that it was the latter. I mean I did have to go to the store at some point and what better time than right then and there. HA! (let's not forget I am a student here).

So let us visit that question again, "what are sources of unsteadiness in my life?" The answer, potentially EVERYTHING and EVERYONE, which is why it is up to me to keep it *up to ME*. The best way I know of doing this is by getting enough sleep/rest. Eating foods that will nourish, not rob me of nutrients. Being kind, accepting, forgiving, and loving of myself. With these elements in place, I will be better equipped to handle those attacks on my inner peace when they hit me blindside. Steady vs Unsteady? The pivotal element is ME.

Steady as She Goes

How can we find steadiness in a world that is constantly spinning? *Steadiness*, in a world in which the moral compass is no longer a directional we can trust for our safety, our well-being, or a secure, sustainable future, *has become a rare commodity.*

The answer, I believe is that we CANNOT find steadiness from an outward source. The world is anything but steady. It is in a state of constant motion of different and conflicting events, ideas, choices, and occurrences. Steadiness can only come from within and can only be placed there by oneself.

My *steadiness* can only come from within and only *I* can place it there, via my thoughts. Anchor it there, via my practice of it, and nurture it, via my appreciation of it. To be steady is a choice. To be steady is a freedom we all are born with. No one can take it from us unless we allow them to. It does require a certain strength of mind and heart to protect it. To keep it from being stolen from us. Because those without it will try. Though they don't realize what they are doing. They *crave* the calm that radiates outward from a soul that is grounded in this solid energy of steadiness. We all inherently require this steadiness to thrive. This need for inner peace is placed there by the Divine.

Therefore, whether steady surrounds me, or chaos, if I desire this *steadiness*, I must place it within myself and I must be careful to protect it.

I believe those who have found their steady ground have an obligation, for the betterment of this very unsteady world we call our home, and the rest of the human race who live among us, to share it, via words of encouragement, via actions of kindness and generosity, and via love with open arms and open hearts directed toward and radiating out into our surroundings and those who crave to be *steady*.

6
SUMMER

Morning Treasures

I went for a walk this morning before beginning my workday, not my usual a couple of blocks and back but rather a long walk.

I felt a pretty good start, a little stiff in the hips and an overall heaviness to my step, but I pressed on.

I did contemplate turning around at my usual stopping place but decided to continue. That's right about when the little blessing treasures began to appear.

The first was when I stopped at an interval when I began to feel thirsty and felt the need to take a drink from the water bottle, I was so thankful I had brought with me. Taking a long sip of the cool water, I noticed I was standing right next to a fire hydrant - I found that ironic and got a chuckle from it.

Laughter is the greatest treasure and health benefit a body could ask for.

The second treasure was when I rounded the corner after the long trek around half of my subdivision when I realized I didn't feel nearly as stiff, and my step felt much lighter. Truly a blessing for someone that suffers from chronic arthritis hip pain. Perseverance produces progress and some pain relief to boot.

I noticed after a while *from the second time I had stopped for a drink from my water bottle* that TIME had not occurred to me, not even once since my walk began. Another blessing for a woman nearing her 60th year, we want *time* to *not* be something we dwell on but rather cherish slowly with enjoyment.

Then came the third and most treasured treasure of all.

A beautiful cardinal flew past my stride, right about the time my mind began to awaken to the fact that - I needed to get to my workday, and right before I arrived back to my street - the blessing I took from the cardinal visiting my path was - do not fret the small stuff.

What I was doing was the best way to start my day, and the blessings of my walk would most certainly spill out over my workday in the most rewarding ways.

So have a great day!

Remember to keep your eyes open for little treasures that present themselves - they can carry the biggest blessings for you to carry out into your day. Oh, and as for work - I was right on time as the cardinal knew I would be.

Music, Smiles, and Generous Hearts

The other day while walking out of Target, I heard music playing. My first thought was that it was coming from a passing car with its tunes playing loudly, but as I approached the parking lot, I saw that it was not coming from a car but a man playing violin on a curb near the entrance. He was there with a young woman. They had a sign that read "out of work, need rent."

It was not the first time this talented young man blessed passersby with his lovely violin playing. He had been there before at least a couple of times when I was there shopping.

I walked to my car and loaded my trunk with my purchases. My mind was combing the contents of my purse, where I usually had some money tucked in various spots. *No, I used that couple of dollars at a local coffee shop, where often, people in need visit.* I got in my car and checked the small compartment on the door I use for loose change that finds its way into my pockets. *Again - nope, not much in there except for a few pennies, nickels, and dimes. That spot also had been emptied at an earlier trip somewhere for a tootsie roll or two while waiting for red to turn to green.*

I started my engine and began to pull out after checking around and behind me. Then a thought came to my mind which hadn't finished scanning my purse contents. I remembered a Dunkin' Donuts gift card that I was pretty sure was unused or had at least a small balance left on it. Otherwise, it would not have remained in my wallet.

So, I decided to walk back to the curbside concert and offer the small token.

Walking back from dropping my hay penny in the bucket beside the musical duo, I noticed people getting out of their cars, looking and pointing toward the melody filling the sky. Smiles were adorning every face that turned their ears toward the sweet sounds, I hoped those smiles were attached to generous hearts. And that an appreciation of the music and the talented gentleman sharing his gift with the masses would spark an adequate return.

His music was an invitation to smile, and those smiles would encourage hearts to open and hands to give.
One blessing leads to another and another until there is plenty to go around.

All sparked by the beautiful gift of music.

Singing Bowls for Healing Souls

Let the sound wash over you

Let its energy vibrate through you

From the top of your head to the tips of your toes

Wake up mind it's a new day

Fluttering eyes take in the beauty that surrounds

Inhale

The sweetness of being alive

Exhale

Any energy that binds

Heart beating in tune with Mother Earth

The universe sustaining

Every breath

A birth

Every exhale

A death

Ebbing and flowing

From ignorance to knowing

Seeing learning growing

Sounds vibrating

Waking your soul

Feel it glowing

Grounded

Ready

Embrace

The day

Let yourself BE

In its flow

The Smell of Rain

The sound of birds.

A cooler summer morning.

The makings of a perfect day.

The birds and critters were seemingly more vocal than what my ears typically hear in the early morning.

Their symphony certainly had a more - *Dom, Dom, Dom,* feel to it.

I thought of recording the stereo sonic sounds of nature that surrounded me. I pondered, if I was ever in a state of being or situation where my great outdoors was not graspable to me, I could play my video recording of this morning's symphony and return to this place of silent, yet sound filled moments.

No longer did the thought flutter across my mind, than the droplets of heavens cleansing began.

Rain.

A steady flow of it.

Explaining the frenzy of noise that was audible just moments before from the birds and critters residing outdoors.

As I sat on my cabin's front porch, my soul took in the smell of the early summer morning's rain. My ears took in the now muffled sounds of the birds and critters as they nestled into branches, shrubs, and grass to shelter from the wetness that fell from the heavens.

As I observed, I relished in the beauty of my surroundings. I felt blessed and so grateful for my home, my family, friends, and all that encompasses my ordinary, *spectacular* life.

And the rains fell and the critters silently slumbered while waiting for the rains to subside, and the candle flickered as I sat on my porch taking it all in.

Ahh...the smell of rain.

The sound of birds.

A cooler summer morning.

The makings of a perfect day.

Myself, Coffee, and a Cat

Nestled on my lap she purrs.

With every lift of the cup to my lip she nudges my hand as if to say

Pet please – NOW.

With the cooler morning, I open a window.

At first, I hear the almost silent sounds of the morning hours.

Those that if your heart is not in tune, you will miss because of all the static that surrounds.

And though my heart and ears remain open to Mother Nature's morning symphony,

still those small sounds become almost distant background noise when the hustle and bustle of the world's morning begins.

I can not only hear but can feel the noise pollution that like a fog rolls in as the day breaks.

There's the sound of the traffic speeding along the highway, rumblings from passing trains.

Sirens and honks,

Engines starting,

Engines revving,

and somewhere in the distance the crow of a rooster attending to his natural early morning ritual of wake-up calls.

Unaware of all the noise that surrounds he continues to shout

I'm still here to crow, so you might hear -

It is time to rise -

Begin your day...

Despite the clanking and clamoring from the break of man's day my ears remain open; my heart remains in tune.

I still enjoy the sounds the morning makes.

I listen to the chirping birds as they greet and make their nests

Good morning, Robin -

Hello to crow -

And all the little critters inching down below...

Mother Nature's alarms are faithfully set,

If we keep our hearts in tune, the almost silent sounds of morning cannot be muffled away by the world's static that attempts to infiltrate our day.

Because despite the world turning,

The rooster still calls —
Time to wake — It's daybreak.

Here's to Birthdays – Past, Present, and Future

Let me turn you back to July 2021. Our family had been through some trying times and it was the 9th of July (my birthday) when my family received the most wonderful news that would mark a *new beginning* for us all.

Feeling completely saturated in gratitude; I wrote this piece. However, in my usual fashion I let the day-to-day grind become front and center and never posted it (on my blog).

My last year's birthday held and will always hold a special place in my heart and although it has now been a full year, and I have already celebrated another birthday - I decided to go ahead and post this piece.

So, turn back one year to 2021 - my birthday.

July 2021:

My birthday was a little over a week ago. This year marked a significant time for our family. The last few years have been full of positive and negative energies for many - our family has been no exception. We have all had to go through some pretty earth-shattering changes but finally, the tide seems to be changing and there is much hope floating through the atmosphere. I feel I can finally breathe, and I am ready for a new day.

I've always been interested and even fascinated in astrology. It is a part of my nature to always be searching out truths and I find there is so much about the energies of our universe and ourselves that are just jaw dropping. A few years ago, I began observing my energy levels and how certain highs and lows seemed to coincide with the phases of the moon. So, I began to read and study a little about it.

Like I said our universe and everything in it fascinates me. So, this year I was delighted to notice that my birthday fell smack dab on the new moon. A time for new beginnings and making commitments to taking steps to make dreams come true.

My birthday, for me, is a new year, so like the traditional new year, I usually make some resolutions and personal goals for myself. This year was no different except that it landed on a new moon so perhaps my goals will have a little more cosmic energy fueling them.

Let's hope. One thing is for sure my birthday brought some wonderful news for our family.

It is certainly a new day, a new time for fresh starts.

And if there is anything holding us back, we can let it all go later this week because at the two weeks past my birthday mark, we get to experience the energy of the full moon. A chance to forgive and let go of anything laying heavy on our minds and in our hearts.

We are all a part of this great cosmic force. We all experience positive energies and negative energies, we all have good moods, bad moods, happy times and sad. But the miracle of it all is that the Creator of this universe has our best interests at heart. He has carved out unique paths for each of us. Paths that are not always straight and are not always smooth. But He never gives us more than we can handle, and He always walks beside us every step of the way. For this I am filled with gratitude abounding. I am in awe and will forever be in search of ways to show and share my gratitude for all that is in my universe - my family, my friends, my work, my plans, my hopes, my dreams.

The sun is shining, the air is warm, and our lives are filled with promise.

I couldn't have asked for a better birthday; I couldn't wish for a more beautiful summer, and I couldn't dream of a better life and for all of this and more I am filled with unimaginable gratitude.

It's like the universe hit the restart button and gave us all a chance to reboot...

and God in His infinite love and mercy, with a wave of His mighty hand, a wink with His watchful eye, changed all the heartache into happy, proving once again - He never gives us more than we can bear and in all things He works for the good of those who love Him and who have been called to His purpose (Rom 8:28).

I very much felt His presence July 9th, 2021, and from the blessings that were bestowed that day, I heard His loving, silent voice whisper ~ Happy Birthday, my dear.

The Music in Your Life

Experience the joy of the music in your life.

Savor the melody you are playing.

Enjoy the rhythm of your day.

Some moments will be in harmony - some a little out of tune but as a whole it is an orchestra.

However, your ensemble comes into form - when it all blends together -

a symphony is born.

Some days are upbeat - others drag along - like a low baritone.

Whatever may be the *tune* of the day - relax and make it your own.

Experience the joy of the music in your life.

Savor the melody you are playing.

Enjoy the rhythm of your day.

We are only given a short time - to play.

Vacation

Sometimes when the pressures of life seem insurmountable, it's good medicine for the soul to take a deeper look to put things in a better perspective.

We are quite small in our world. *Our* universe is but a spec in God's, yet he views our every need as though it was the hugest, He sees, and He CAN move mountains.

We simply must BELIEVE.

Take a vacation. Get away from it all. Put your troubles and your worries into a perspective you can see, then leave them all to God, and believe.

Worship and Praise

Thank you for the sunshine

Thank you for the breeze

Thank you for the flowers

Thank you for the trees

For every single creature

That creep, that crawl, that slide

Thank you for this earth

Full of wonder and surprise

And with everything that comes along

There's nothing new under the sun, we know

It's all a part of a master plan

For every woman, child, and man

For every shower of rain

That fills a gray day

A rainbow shows its color through the clouds

During winter blizzards, hurricanes of fall

Summer's beating sun

Torrential rains of spring

We find protection

We find safety

Under Your protective wings

We find a cooling calm that shades us from it all

There is no dimension

Nowhere in time or space

That we can ever be hidden

From the light of Your saving grace

So, thank you for the sunshine, even when our skies are gray

Every day is a beautiful day

To worship and to praise

Birthdays

A day of gratitude.

A day to feel blessed and be thankful simply to be alive.

This morning, I woke up to another day. Just your typical, ordinary day except that today is *my birthday* and just the fact that I am having one is enough to make me feel elated.

Now, at my age (somewhere between the top of the hill but not quite to the bottom) most people stop celebrating birthdays because it is a symbol of aging, a reminder of our impending, (well), end of birthdays.

I will admit that in the past (before I decided it is high time I love myself), I didn't make too much ado about birthdays (mine that is), but now that I am older, wiser and able to see clearer (even though I need my specs), I view birthdays as the most glorious gifts because in the last few very short years too many of my loved ones stopped having theirs.

So today I awoke to another day. But not just a typical, ordinary day, because today is *my* birthday.

And at my age with the alternative being *under the ground* - I'll take *over the hill* any day!

7
PULLING WEEDS

Why This Lord?

Why all these things
that has happened to me
Why have you allowed to be
Is it a test to prove
I will be devoted to you
I pray that I do
I hope that my heart remains unhardened

The last two upheavals
I thought more than I could bear
Each had characteristics
Something personal that would shake me to my core
Knock me off my horse
Where I thought the ride was smooth

But you saw me through the roughness
To a place where I could learn
And so I survived doing the best I could do
And yes, you granted us the most mercy we could have ever

known
For which I will be forever grateful and in awe

But this time Lord
This time
You might as well have lit the match
than if the Devil had himself
To set my flesh on fire
While watching my heart melt

My brain may tell me to run and stop relying on humankind
There is too much hurt in this world
I think I would rather die
I may never understand the reason for this; my worst day ever
A title I gave each that passed and thought they would be the last
Never say never
But here I face again
Another course of dread
Will it never end

I no sooner get back up on that horse
Steer my attention towards another course
My stomach kicked again
My breath exits my lungs
Dizziness fills my head
Another jolt I must face
How many lessons must I learn
At least I have the calm, cool of your grace

To comfort me through the burn

I pray this be the last of my life's lessons class
that I am required to attend
As my strength and wits near their end
But then I may be a pile of dust
In the bottom of an urn
And only as I cross through the gate
will I know
if *sufficient*, were the lessons learned

Discipline

...something of late, I have been lacking.

Over the last few years, I have been lax in the practice - of discipline. Self-discipline, to be exact. Using discipline with my diet, exercise, consistency in writing and making art, and my responsibilities concerning some of the groups I'm involved with.

But, while being lax in those areas, I have gotten much better in some other areas, for example, clearing out household clutter of old paperwork, staying on the course with paying off bills, except December - LOL, and keeping up with the pet's yearly vaccinations and check-ups.

So where am I going with this, you may be wondering?
My point is simple. I keep on trying. I keep on starting over. I keep making plans even if I don't always follow through. I keep on moving forward even though I often stumble.

We are again at a New Year starting point, and as in the past years, I have chosen a NEW word to be a reminder of what I hope to strive for and towards in the next 365 days that lie before me. Last year, I chose the word NEW, and I did and experienced a ton of NEW.

Though worry, exhaustion, and anxiety were a part of some of the NEW I experienced, in the end, it was all well worth it when I gained the new title of Grandma.

There was a renewal of faith, hope, and trust.

I found a new sense of accomplishment by stepping out of my comfort zone and learning that sharing in front of an audience was not nearly as scary as I thought it would be. It turns out I enjoy it, AND plans are underway to continue doing more of the same this year.

I have allowed myself to branch out and unearth areas of growth I did not know were possible. Hopefully, with the dawn of next year, I will be singing my praises concerning twenty-twenty-four's word DISCIPLINE.

The Gift of Me

Chisel off the layers of limitations that have accumulated upon my soul.

From a world of negative energies

and untrue stories told.

The Lord so lovely wove me to be the gift that I am.

Help me, Lord, to find her underneath the layers of crap.

I know there is a light that beckons from deep within.

Temping me to be the woman

That my child self knows she is.

To shine like the gem that my soul was born to be.

To live each day with an intention

unafraid to grab those dreams

when the universe unfolds them

open my eyes to see.

Chisel off the layers

to expose the gift of

me.

Blame

It gets tossed from place to place

But often does not find its home

In the rightful *space*, the blame belongs

Sometimes that *space* is the very *place* the blame originally formed

Sometimes we only have ourselves

To blame

Let that rest for awhile

The result may be a happier place for all

Stuff It

Eventually you will absorb the abhor, keep the slant upward

On your lips that is

Don't let anyone be the wiser

Keep your step light

If you feel your busting at your seams

Wait until the moon shines bright

Weep, yourself to sleep at night

Eventually you will absorb the abhor

Making room to stuff some more

Take the Extra Mile

You may notice the scenery is much nicer

Once you step away from your box

Though comfortable as it may be

Until you venture out a bit

See what there is to see

You'll never know what you're capable of

Or how it feels to live FREE

You may run into some bumps along the way

And you won't always have the clearest view

Of what lies ahead for you

But whatever is in store will always hold more

Then the box you left behind

Take the extra mile

You may be surprised to find

The person that was once in the box

Is much happier after stepping outside

Breaking Down Walls

To be truly free you must remove the shell that you have strategically placed around your frame (metaphorically speaking of course)

All this protection of your *physical frame - your shell*

Has caused a vulnerability of your *frame of mind*

You have placed rigidity to protect your core self

You have placed apathy to protect your emotional health

All this protection has the opposite outcome from the desire for which you strive

It removes protection from both your body and mind

Because it isn't only the good people and the pleasant experiences that are needed for a safe, sound life

It's the heartaches, disappointments, and shitty people that we encounter -

That shapes our characters and strengthens our resilience

So ultimately a life full of its share of hurt gives us the stamina to weather the storms that make us our strong selves

Building walls to protect yourself from these normal things of the human experience will be the very thing that breaks you

Don't build walls

Wear your heart on that sleeve for everyone to see

Let your vulnerabilities be the beacon of your light

Break down those walls and be strong -

Open and in plain sight

H.E Double Toothpicks!!!

I am Sorry for Damning You to Hell
And I *will* apologize

I couldn't today because I was too focused on licking my own wounds
I failed to see, you had been lacerated too

Your words cut deep into my flesh

The flesh I keep hidden from everyone

Including myself

I see through my barrier

My heart knows full well

ALL that I am *not*

But learning that *you* see all my empty

Makes me want to run

To hide from your eyes

They pierce me with their look

They see through my disguise

Your heart knows my every lie
Which is how your words hold the power
To bring me down

Mean Spirited

We have all met them.

Those people who find it necessary to knock you off your good mood.

Those who make others feel uncomfortable and uncertain of letting their vulnerabilities show, for fear of giving ammunition to a *never-ending-wound-wielding* array of words, used to abuse.

Those emotional bullies that use sarcasm to bruise, without *the physical* punch to their victims, the impact of the blow being just as damaging.

They use these tactics to make themselves feel strong.

It only illuminates their weakness.

Habitual Progress

It's Habit Forming

Don't do something just out of habit. Do it because it's the best possible way of doing it. *Then keep looking for an even better way.*

We form habits, good and bad. We make rules to keep the good ones. We make plans to rid us of the bad. Well, rules are made to be broken or at the very least, be bent.

We are constantly trying to re-define our boundaries. What is right today is wrong tomorrow. Once taboo, is now ok. Will we ever get it right? Will we ever stop trying to change? There's a lot to be said for mediocre. Not too much, too little, but just right.

I guess it's our human nature to want to keep trying to fix things that aren't broken. And I think that is good (at least to an extent). I mean why settle? If there is any question at all that a different way, a newer way could be better, why not try it? Why just assume the same ole, same ole is the best and only?

Every generation tries to shake things up. Try new ways of doing the same old tasks. Well, that's just as it should be. Would the previous generation have just taken their elder's word for it? No, and they didn't. Nor do any. We all try to change things up. Make things better.

That is what progress is.
And,
it's habitual.

Be Happy or Die Trying

Stop wasting days picking apart what is (*in your opinion only*) wrong with you.

Simply embrace, live, give a big hug to the uniquely beautiful person you are.

It is no mistake, everything, everyone, good, bad, and the ugly, that have come in and out of your life - was for a purpose.

The purpose *which is* your journey, *and* theirs.

It is unique.

It is one of a kind.

It is, was, and will be, for the learning, the growing, the bringing up you - to the exact spot you are right now.

As well as everyone your life in some way touched.

To the children you were, are, or will be, blessed to raise up.

To the person you smiled at, opened the door for, let go ahead of you when they didn't have a cart at the store.

Every moment has played an integral part.

So, stop.

I said stop!

Thinking that somehow anything that wasn't great was your mistake.

And anything that was super good was from *someone else's* should.

Own your life in its entirety and be proud.

Be happy.

Be sad.

Give yourself a pat on the back.

And a swift kick in the saddle bag. (but only when needed)

Because it is all relevant.

It is life.

It is yours.

It is theirs.

It is now.

So be happy -

Or die trying.

Who is Holding Your Joystick?

Get a visual.

You are a warrior.

Always in combat.

Your only opponent,

Is, you.

Why?

You are the pilot.

You are the one in control from your head all the way down to your toes.

You hold the joystick,

In this game of life.

So, get a visual.

You are standing, fully equipped with everything you need to progress.

To be safe, to be healthy, to be happy,

You hold all the controls.

They are at your disposal to do as you will with.

You can continue to control your own life, body, mind,

Or you can hand the controller over to someone, *something* else, time after time.

Now, someone comes along who wants to ultimately control your life because they have lost control of their own.

They say mean things about you,

In an attempt, to knock you off - the throne

That *they* set you upon in their own self sabotaging mind.

Are you going to hand over to them, your joy

Or refuse and say, "it's mine."

Now, someone comes along, and they want to hurt your body,

By stepping into your space.

Bringing energies which at the lowest level,

is the highest they vibrate.

They want to pull you along.

You become their lifeline.

They must feed off your energy,

Because they continually drain their own.

Remember you still have the control.

You can make a choice.

Let them deplete you,

Or stay plugged into your own positive pull.

Let them deplete you,

Or remain energetically full.

Now, imagine a *something* that shows up on your countertop.

You can choose to keep it for stash,

Or you can choose to toss it - it's trash.

Your habits are yours and yours alone to make.

They are also yours to keep or to break.

Only you can make the turn.

Kick the junkie to the curb.

Remember sugar is sweet.

It's not forbidden to eat.

But your fix should come from the sweet that grows on trees,

And isn't the root cause of diabetes.

Again, the control is in your hand.

Leave the cookies in the bag.

You are a warrior.

Not a junk food slave.

You have control,

Over what you crave.

What will be your vice?

Those that enhance life?

Or those that help dig graves?

Get a visual.

You are a warrior.

Always in combat.

Your opponent, you.

Why?

Back to Routine

For quite some time now I have suspected that my motivation is determined by my mood. I suspect there is a definite correlation between my frame of mind and my productivity, or I should say, the lack of it.

At the beginning of this year, I decided to take real action at being productive. I finally admitted to myself that *I* was the only one standing in my way, and so I decided to do something about it so that I can finally get things done. By getting out of *my own* way I can begin to do some things that I have been wanting to do and that will ultimately move me closer to my dreams becoming my reality.

Having made this decision, I began the task of implementing new habits with respect to blessing my home and my hobbies (passions), with the intention that as my spaces become more comfortable and as I begin scheduling the "to do's" that will directly move my dreams forward, I will ultimately be a much happier and fulfilled person.

However, I also know that although I am basically a very optimistic person and usually see the glass half full more than half empty, there are times when my mood plummets and with it my productivity goes way down too.

This usually occurs without warning.
So being prepared will save me from my own derailment.
Right?
Read on.

Knowing this about myself, as I said earlier, I have been keeping a more careful eye on my productivity and mood connection. Sure-enough I got the proof I needed.

And here it is.

I was moving right along with my newfound routines and feeling great about my productivity when SLAM something struck me down.

I received a phone call from a family member, (a close one, not one I could simply ignore), and the call quickly became the emotional *dump on me session*, that it always seems to become.

Now I was aware of my suspicions (mood and motion), so I told myself - NO this time I was not going to let it throw me out of balance. Just let, so and so, vent and then go on your merry way.

Well guess what?
It did (*throw me out of balance*).

The thought had barely finished crossing my mind when I could feel the effect of that phone call on my physical body *and* my mood. It dropped, right into that familiar gutter of my mind, taking my battered heart with it. And since then, my productivity has continued dragging along in the ditch.

Damn, I did it again. I could write a song about it, or rather I let someone else do it again. Throw me out of my happy place right back into my, *guilt ridden, I'm the blame of it all, you really suck as a person, yada, yada, yada place*. And *that* is the place - I now know for certain, is the birthplace of my unproductive ways.

So, it has been about three weeks, and not one but two - three phone calls of the same nature and text messages too. And what have I noticed? My productive "new habits" are dwindling. Yes, I am clutching on to a couple of the REALLY IMPORTANT habits that I have managed to implement, but little by little they will float away to. Back into the fog of depression and despair. The place I all too often find myself looking around and wondering why can't I simply get it together and do the things my heart desires and stick to my own plans?

Well, I have answered that question. Most definitively, without a doubt. The real question is how to stop the cycle so that I can stop being thrown off my course. How do I *not* let other's moods affect my mood?

The most logical answer I could come up with is - It can't be done.

The only thing that *can* be done is to not let it negatively affect my groove.

Besides making sure others know that from this point on, I simply refuse to be their human emotional dartboard. Regardless, since they are sure to get a few darts launched at me before I even get the words out, I just must *feel* the way I feel, take a little (I stress little), time to lick my wounds (without deepening the cut with my own negative reactions to what was done, said, or texted). Remind myself that those words and actions come from the place *they are in* (or rather *stuck*), not from the place I am presently in.

I am not going to define myself by someone else's definition of me.

And when I am ready, I'll get on with the tasks at hand. I'll say a little prayer for those that are hurt and carry on with those things that are important for *me* to reach my goals - my dreams.

I will make a conscious decision to do this - right away - before my train of thought and motion gets derailed again. It is so hard to get back on track. So, I must not add to the derailment. Instead, I'll just take a short break, sit on the track for a while doing nothing, then get right back to rolling along.

Bird's Eye View

When a thought comes to mind that causes you a pang, step out of the scene for a moment, just simply step away. Hang back and observe.

Now ask yourself the question, what good does this thought really serve?

In taking yourself out of the emotion, you will notice, "none" is the only logical answer.

So "out" of your mind the thought ought to go. Keep those scenarios that pop in your mind on a more positive note.

This same technique will be useful when faced with those real-life dramas that often pop up with people in your life, who frequently come and go. They usually show up unexpected and with the sole intent of an emotional unload.

When you are faced with a confrontation YOU did not choose. Stop the scene, meditatively speaking. Push your snooze. Step away from the conflict, go to your birds' eye view, and ascertain the direction your body, your voice should choose to best serve the others, the whole situation, but mostly YOU.

You see observing from outside of the *scene*, you get a better view, of the truth and the best direction you should take is more clearly seen, maybe not by them, but certainly by you.

You're more able to make the better choice. *Before* your actions, *before* your voice.

Leaving less feathers ruffled in the air. Leaving less baggage sprawled all about, and more importantly, leaving far less, regret for you to fret about.

Our own negative self-talk, and the battles we wage against ourselves within the realm of our psyche can be as, if not more, damaging than actual drama and confrontations with the people in our lives. And just as daily meditation can keep us in check with our emotions to be mentally equipped to handle those situations with others, taking a meditative approach to recognizing and combating our negative and wrong thinking pattern *scenes* we create in our minds, can be life changing as well.

Our well-being depends on many factors, the way we take care of our bodies, the daily interactions we have with others, *and* the daily communication we have with ourselves too - within our thoughts, the way we feel. But mostly the way we allow those thoughts and feelings to dictate the directions we take.

Do, think, and feel with the clear intent of "I want to be happy, I want to feel good" or even better, "I AM happy, I DO feel good", is a sure-fire way to BE the BEST YOU - *for you.*

Revisions

You can't close one book, open another with the same information, same words, same stories that were in the first book and expect any difference in the end.

You must rewrite it.

You must take out the negative words and replace them with positive.

You must strip all the lies that it's been filled with and replace those lies with facts.

By doing this you will change the whole feel of the story (*your story - you*).

If you are naturally wired to be a little OCD, with perfectionist habits locked in place,

Uncross the wires.

Rewire your thinking so that your existence becomes brighter and more focused.

Stop living in the dark.

Stop struggling to get through each day with only your dimmers leading the way.

Stop the cycle.
Make a real change.

Rewrite your story.
Create it to be great.

The Silent Treatment

At the end of the day, it's not about what a person is doing to you. It's more about what *you* are doing to be the person you want to be.

Don't let another's lack of, be the measure of *your* integrity.

Don't react. And certainly, don't *overreact*.

Just take a moment or two (if needed), to choose *your* best response. And know that in some cases that may be - none.

There is a lot to be said for - NO response.

In the end it's you that you must face in the mirror. And it's your inner voice that will be pecking at your ear with murmurs of regret.

So, stay true to the person *you* want to be.

And know, that may mean to simply - not speak.

A lot can be heard in - *silence*.

The Remedy

No healing comes from guilt and blame
Only out of forgiveness can a new beginning dawn
Growth will follow once we allow
Ourselves to forget and move on

And that seems to be the hard part. The *moving on*. No matter how hard we try, we seem to be programmed to replay repeatedly in our minds, the very memories we want to forget. We seem to keep looking under our emotional bandages, exposing the very wounds we are trying not to pick.

Blame, guilt, unforgiving, are all symptoms from a heart diseased with HURT.

And *we* are our own worst enemies, not the villains in our minds. We *want* to change the bad habits that keep us from getting over our hurts, but *we* place our minds on the coals, that carry the smolder to burn. We must lay to rest the old favorite past time of reminiscing with our negative thoughts. It's the ego that likes to remind us of those that did us wrong. But the spirit holds the wisdom, and it lies within us all. It's the essence of our existence. From the Divine - a call - to open our closed minds to the promise of a *new heart* song.

We are our good physicians. *We* have the remedies we need. *We* can eliminate the pain. *We* can cure the disease.

Every pain we experience, every good, every bad, e-v-e-r-y-thing. It is all meant for a purpose. It's needed for us to hurt, to mend, to sooth, to sting, to cry, to sing, *and* to die. It's ALL needed for us to evolve into the beings we were born to be.

Step outside of the view of *self*. Look on as a spectator would. You may discover by doing so, more clearly are these truths understood. When a thought comes to mind that brings with it a feeling of angst, step out of the scene for a moment, just simply step back and observe. Now ask yourself the question "what good does this thought serve?" By taking yourself out of the emotion, you're more able to live in the NOW, where all the past's bad memories no longer hold any ground.

Ultimately, we must rely on trust. A deep knowledge that all will be well.

Forgiveness, acceptance, understanding, and love are the only remedies that work, to relieve the symptoms and ultimately cure, our hearts diseased from HURT.

Mind Set – Reset

When my gut starts aching, I know some serious *gutting* needs to take place.

Negative thinking. Worry. Limits. Fear. We inherit these from practically the day we are born. And like our bodies, these tendencies, grow bigger and stronger with every passing year, ultimately wreaking havoc in our bodies and our lives. Until finally we hit a dead end and realize, like I recently have that...

My entire belief system needs a remodel if it's ever going to fit the expansive needs of my universe.

Because my life IS as big as the universe. The sky is the limit! Whatever I desire my life to be, I can achieve. The secret of course is to *believe*.

See it in the distance. Think it into existence.

The Law of Attraction. Yes, I DO believe!

Why then is this invisible mental block constantly restricting me? How can I shift what I believe in my heart, into my head?

Perhaps the answer lies in consistency. It may just be that the mind (aka ego), may never be in sync with the heart. It's quite possible that the human spirit will forever be in a battle of the wits with the cerebral part of our essence.

The secret might be to simply *ignore* when you hear "I can't" from a *mind* screeching and with the spirit, *just keep on reaching*.

Don't Rain on My Parade

Sometimes no matter how bright and sunny your day is, someone else's dark cloud seems to find you.

We all have our days where everything just seems to fall out of place. And when that happens a good rule of thumb is to take a step back before you go tumbling completely off track and do a gratitude check.

Gratitude checks are a great way to put your bad day into perspective.

Maybe it's not a bad day overall. Maybe there are some things you sailed right through. Check in with yourself and determine just how bad a day is it - really? Then, and no matter what determination you come up with, thank the universe for both the bad parts of the day and the good.

Now there are times and days when even after doing all this and positioning yourself back on the track of *sunny disposition*, inevitably someone who is also having a bad day, comes along and brings their dark cloud right along with them, dousing you with a downpour of their negative vibe.

Clearly, they did not do a gratitude check.

It's true there are those that take some sort of pleasure in directing their *frustrations of self* onto others, but I would say for the vast majority, it is simply unintentional.

Frustrations build, causing fumes of anger to form, and sometimes without warning - it all explodes - emotional shrapnel hitting anyone who happens to be in its way.

The best thing to do is to remove yourself, at least temporarily, away from the detonation to let the ash fall, then offer kindness to cool off any remaining smoldering and ever so gently steer them toward getting back on their track by helping them shift into a more positive place of *gratitude*.

If it Works, Keep Working it!

I have decided that going forward before I do anything I will ask myself a question, "Is this working for me?" If the answer is "yes", then I will carry on. If the answer is "no", then I will let it go.

We develop practices, which help us keep our lives in balance. Some of which worked well in the past but may no longer work now. Out of habit, we continue to do the same things, though, clearly, they are *not* working and could be the reason for our feeling out of balance.

These practices we develop become *patterns* which feel familiar to us. They become our comfort zone where we feel safe. This makes change even harder because it feels scary. We are just too scared to want to change the patterns we have created. To break out of our *familiar*. Not knowing what awaits us in the *unknown*, we don't want to go. But to change is necessary if we are to grow.

Don't be afraid to venture on a different path. Learn to recognize that sometimes things that worked in the *past*, may no longer work, in the *now*. It's an ever-changing world and our lives are ever-changing in it. Therefore, we need to be open to change with it.

You can lie to yourself and claim that you are perfectly happy just to stay where you are but look around you. Are there signs that maybe you're NOT?

I have found that whenever I get into a rut and become tired of the same old daily grind, it shows in my appearance, my household, my projects, relationships, everything.

When you have unfinished projects scattered around. When clutter replaces organization. When you feel overwhelmed by tasks that you used to breeze through. You might be in a rut. Your life could be out of balance. Your patterns may be wrinkled. And your comfort zone, where you safely sit watching the world go around *without ever climbing aboard*, could be stifling the atmosphere you breathe every day and limiting your growth.

Get up and go for a walk. Turn on some music, play it in the house - loud. Call a friend and chat for a while. Do anything to break up the day. You'll feel refreshed with a new sense of purpose. You'll likely feel motivated to start where you so many times have left off.

The important thing is to keep changing your day up when you start to feel it dragging you down. Keep your life feeling fresh, keep your mind refreshed, keep doing your day at your best.

If it works, keep working it but if it doesn't let it go. Don't be afraid to change it up *and grow*.

Self-Sabotage

When self-sabotage is driving me crazy, moderation is the key.

If I control my choices, why am I a puppet to my habits? My self-sabotage habits. They are the axle of the self-destructive roller coaster ride that I keep jumping on.

One step forward, three steps back. It seems with this sequence I've developed a knack.

I'm sure I'm not alone here. You feel miserable yet you keep repeating the same behaviors that make you feel miserable.

Today I just want to run (though I'm pretty sure I would get winded), to the nearest fat farm to DETOX. I ate sugar yesterday and that carried right into today, as it always does. It must STOP. I keep telling myself. I *must* take off the extra weight I've put on. I felt so good after losing it, why do I keep forgetting, or rather, ignoring how I put it on in the first place?

How many of you out there are having the same conversations, with yourselves?

I just want to *literally* have my cake and eat it too. I want to enjoy all the goodies, *but* I must realize that a choice must be made. Now, of course, there is that little thing called, moderation. I have yet to master that. So, for myself at least I must decide - EAT the muffin top and HAVE the muffin bottom or eat LEAN and be TRIM.

Making the choice is easy. I mean really, it's a no brainer, right? The hard part is sticking to the choice you make. We live in a society where we are bombarded with too many choices available. A society of literally too much where so many unhealthy habits can develop, taking hold of an addictive personality. *Figuratively speaking*, the effects of eating a pastry will cling to my thighs, and so too will the *desire* to have one *take root* in my mind. We have so much to choose from it can promote overindulgence in our habits.

How many of us can admit to finding an article of clothing or SHOES, you just love, and they fit so right, that you buy multiple colors of the same item? And with online shopping not only can we do it without having to move our fannies, but we can do it with discounts, coupons, and free shipping, to sweeten the *crave* even more.

So, it isn't just about eating too much cake. It's too much everything. And if you are in an all or nothing mindset, self-sabotage is almost inevitable.

I can only speak for myself, but I think it takes a constant shifting of gears. If you find yourself parked in that all or nothing mindset, make a shift to first decide *not* to over-do. Second, watch out for those familiar signs. When the need for a cookie hits you head on, yield, check your mirrors (especially the rear view) and proceed with caution. The impulse may hit you hard but if you STOP, the damage will be minimal, and you'll be glad you didn't total out your day. With practice, your mindset will be more neutral rather than *all or nothing*.

Keep turning your focus back towards your goal where moderation is the key. Stop the self-sabotage. Cut those puppet strings.

You − Control = Trust

To Sum Up, It's a Matter of *Trust*

"If I can't control what happens to me, what is left?" My daily reading asked this question, and my immediate response was TRUST. If you believe in a Higher Power (for me it is God), then that answer seems the only one.

Believing in this Higher Power gives us faith and with faith, trust should come easy. Well, let's be honest, *trust* is something easier said than done. It is our human nature, to want to hold on to *control*, as futile as it is, we think we possess such power. However, accepting that you have no control over what happens to you is key, though it is not a realization that comes easy for most. It takes humility.

There are some angels among us that I believe are literally born with humble hearts and for them, faith and trust come as effortlessly as taking a breath. But for most of the inhabitants of this planet, it does not come so easy. I would consider myself in the latter group. For these, such as myself, humility must chisel its way through the dense walls of pride. It takes a Power with an unyielding amount of patience and love to place that chisel at the precise angle to reflect in the most illuminating light the many facets of each individual and to apply the right amount of pressure and intensity, to sculpt masterpieces out of our hard exteriors.

But when the humble heart begins to shine forth, we are enlightened with the realization that only with complete abandonment of the need to control do we find true freedom. Free from the craving to control our surroundings we find the *fruit of freedom* which is TRUST.

Is What You See Merely How YOU Perceive?

You can't determine your life's worth by whether someone answers a phone call!

Is what you see merely how you perceive? I learned today that my reaction to a situation that occurs more frequently than it ever should in my world, over the years has been dulled. An episode which would normally cause an extreme upset and did for a family member who had never been exposed, no longer has the same effect on me. And frankly, that scares the hell out of me.

The irony in this is that it is precisely a matter of perception that caused the issue in the first place. To even walk the slippery slope of perception, assuming, and reading between lines that have been drawn in mind only, can and will lead to a dark world where negativity is the only energy being spent. Ask the three questions, am I seeing clearly? Am I acting generously? Am I accepting what I can't change? (Taken from "The Daily Stoic Journal", by Ryan Holiday).

Being honest with ourselves can be very difficult. We are all struggling. We are all guilty of not taking much time for those we love. But it never means we don't love. Drawing conclusions without gathering REAL facts will never lead to solutions. It only causes more problems. More drama, more pain.

My lesson today had to do with Perception, Action, and Will. In the universe's expertise, my day aligned to just that frequency. I was given a gift to see how another's perception led to emotional pain, which resulted in someone being hurt and upset and how that, in turn, was perceived by yet another. I was able to realize that perhaps I need to be kinder in my actions to individuals who have difficulty with their perception in a world they unknowingly trap themselves in. And finally, how grateful I am that everything is once again calm.

Taken from The Daily Stoic, words I am striving to live by..."All you need are these: certainty of judgement in the present moment; action for the common good in the present moment; and an attitude of gratitude in the present moment for anything that comes your way."

I think I'll share them with others.

8
MEMORIES

Hometown Joliet

Taking chances doesn't come easily for me. But recently, *encouraged by some very special people in my life*, I took a big one. One of the requirements was to write a poem about a city. It took a bit for me to craft just the right words, but eventually they began to pour. Below is the outcome of my word flow. Now for technical reasons, I couldn't carry through to the end - with the *chance* but having taken it at all was a huge win for me.

and now here is my poem -

Hometown
Joliet

What does this city mean to me?
To be quite honest,
the thought had never really occurred,
not unlike many, I took it for granted, you see
until that is, just recently.

When an opportunity opened itself,
to be a part of something new,
to which I now find myself humbled to present this poem for you.

For the last few weeks, I have been pondering
and embarked on some Google wandering
in search of city history.
Perhaps a mystery.
Anything to assist in answering the question

What does this city mean to me?

I looked at how this town has grown
To things from the past
and projects developing now.
But the words
somehow
were still escaping.

So, deciding to look within
I peeled the onion, so to speak.
Through layers that define,
buried deep, I found elements of time
to reveal - the ME.

Reasons why unfolding
Writer's block unloading
Words rushed to mind
Just like that – a little at a time

It was simple after all
How to verbalize
What our city means to me
When I let my foggy mind focus on *my family tree.*

What does Joliet mean to ME
As a person
As an individual born here,
Raised in a family with firmly planted roots?

The answer to the question was not in the *what*, or *why*
but in the WHO
is where I would find.

So, I began a new search
In my memories
which I am honored to share.

So - what does Joliet mean to me?

Home

It is where I was born
The place I still call home

Family

In this quaint canal town
and the area that surrounds
Our family roots run deep in the ground

My mom and her sisters (four in all),
when they were young women starting out

they worked right here downtown.

They waited tables for the old Woolworth Restaurant lunchtime crowd.
My Aunts told the stories of the people they would see,
while serving them lunch or an afternoon tea.

I remember just loving to hear them tell.
Thinking back makes my heart swell.

The next to the oldest, named Anna May, was a beautician.
She put herself through school to learn her trade.
As a woman,
she was well beyond the times,
some might say.

She even opened her own business
Ann's Beauty Shop - was the name
We Curl Up and Dye for You - was the game

Located on Chicago Street
right in the heart, the center of the city.

Growing up, I did not realize,
That she was one of the trailblazers
of her time.

Today,
I feel proud
that deep within my roots
my family was an intricate part
of the fabric that weaves the story of this town.

my *Heritage*

Italian and Slovenian immigrants settled here to begin
something of their own.
And from their many descendants, I am blessed
to also call this city my home.

As a young girl
our family attended mass
at St Joseph Parish,
a timeless treasure of stone and stained glass.

I remember being amazed by the beauty of the ceilings and arches
filled with breathtaking art.
I fell in awe as a young girl, then
and still do today when I attend
a special mass for family or friend.

Although raised on the farther west side,
our family went downtown from time to time.
The Rialto Theater was the place to be
for a matinee show in a balcony seat.
Today, it is quite the concert scene.

Like many in the nation, our city has seen ups and downs.
Lean years came,
bringing financial pangs.
The generation of today know not the names
as once iconic stores
were forced to close their doors.

But the heart of the city kept a faint beat.
With dedication and pride
over time
our city with its tarnished edges
began again to shine.

A few years in the making
just look at all that is shaking.
Restaurants, museums, and a new venue for music, too.

YES!

See us, Forge, ahead.

Rounding the corner, enjoy some summer fun
while cheering in the stadium for a Slammer big home run.

Yes!

we have our very own baseball team
housed in our state-of-the-art field.
How much cooler can we get?
Even famous people like Bill Murray
and the Veecks
think that Joliet
is a sure bet.

History

Museums,
Landmarks
A prison over a century old

Theaters like Billie Limacher Bicentennial Park
and, of course, The Rialto
at our city center heart.

A city rich in *Architecture*

Central School,
a mansion, or two
Just look at the beauty of the old train station,
the downtown library,
and the spectacular campus of USF
to name just a few

In the cathedral area where the streets are lined, with pride
With gorgeous homes that have stood the test of time
Centered among The Cathedral of St Ray,
never looking better than today

The old Joliet Prison
Once housed men who met their fate
When they became inmates of the state

Those walls now echo a different tune
As it once was a score and soon-to-be encore
When a couple of good old Brothers
called it home to sing some blues

The old and once-abandoned prison
Now hosts historical landmark tours
And soon to be much more
Its history and many others

make up our city core

Support

A community that cares
Men, women, children
Some of which are in dire need
Find resources here

Because of mentors,
big sisters, big brothers,
organizations that provide
stepping-stones to pull people up,
give them tools to rise above
to not only survive,
but to do so and thrive

What gives our city its flare?

I believe it is the people,
the rich history of lives shared
our city reflects the essence of a community
of folks who genuinely care.

Of course, meaning and importance vary for each who has called
Joliet home.
Unique for every set of footsteps that walk along its streets.
Not unlike how our hearts resonate
from the elements we see in art.
Nuances that reflect in our identity
make us feel and give us a meaning to do our part.

Everyone has reasons of their own
why they feel blessed to call this city home.

After some pondering and a little Google wandering
it led me to venture into the deep
To fully uncover and peel back the reasons
this city of Joliet means so much to me.

When I looked past what and why
I uncovered family pride.
Reliving memories of my family and my youth
I realized it was the WHO.

It is the people that make up the sweet ingredients
the recipe for any town to flourish.

From our past, in our present, and far into the future
Both young and old
A beautiful blending of souls -
For a city
to be called,
a home.

Home

When I think of *home*
I think of Mom
A cozy little house
On a quaint little street
Where a whole family grew up
Over the years some would remain
Some would leave
I think of soup
In an old butter bowl
With crackers neatly buttered
On a napkin's fold
I think of days off of school
Lying sick on the couch
With Mom cooking in the kitchen
And busy all around the house
She made our house so nice
So comfy so warm
She was always smiling and cheerful
Rarely did she scorn
When I think of *home*
I think of meals prepared
On a green colored stove
Her favorite color, for anyone who didn't know
Breakfasts and lunches
Supper every night
And us, seated at a table
The whole family of five

Cookies would bake for every holiday
Or even just to have for a snack
And especially when dad ran out of malted milk balls, chocolate stars, ice cream, and goodies like that
Christmas with extended family
Hearing jingles on the roof
And Santa came every year
Whether naughty or good
Store bought birthday cakes
In those days a rare treat
Now a day it's all anybody eats
Thanksgiving had to be the best
Just a relaxing day with us, her only guests
Waking up to the smell of turkey
She had stuffed in the wee hours
Just so that by noon
Her family could devour
She always set the table nice
With the china that she loved
Thanksgiving was the only day
She allowed it to be touched
Now that we're all grown
With the grandkids in tow
So many evenings we would visit
To watch favorite shows
Barely hearing the tele
While conversation flowed
"I'm headed to Louise's"
Would be my cue

What a blessing to have your mom living right next door to you
We would sit for hours gabbing, venting, with lots of laughing too
Always staying way too late
Oh how I am going to miss those precious hours
Now that I have run out of those precious days
At the time, not realizing, how special they were
Until now when we no longer have
Her
And I haven't even had time
To just sit home and cry
But the tears keep coming
Whether time allows, or not
I just wish they could bring with them
More time with my mom
When I think of *home*
I think of Mom
No longer there
And my heart feels empty and bare
She left just a couple weeks ago
To tend to our eternal home
She will keep it cozy and warm
And fill our hearts with love
While she mothers from above
Still
I'll be forever sad
At the loss of both, my mom and dad
Though every time I enter my childhood home
I'll feel anything but all alone

For memories there surround me
A few bad but mostly all good
When I think of *home*
I will always think of Mom
Who did exactly as a good mother, should
And the best any woman ever could
She lived as an angel, a saint
Patient and *giving* right up to the last breath she could take
With sparkling tears in her eyes
Her love for us all was shown
When I think of Mom I'll think of an ordinary house
She lovingly made
Our home

Cosmic Connections

I find it curious that recently on at least three different occasions when dialing our office number to retrieve voicemails, I begin entering my telephone number on the touchpad. Why is it that, suddenly, I am attempting to dial myself? I cannot remember any other time when this occurred. Similarly, on several occasions when I needed to write, type, or verbally state my address rather than the number 2417 (my actual address), I have written, typed, or spoken the number 2421 (my childhood home address).

We built our home next to my mother's, the same house I grew up in with my sister and brother. After mom passed on, my brother and sister-in-law moved into the home. So, I still spend a lot of time there.

With my mind fluttering to my past and my fingers dialing my telephone number, is my subconscious trying to connect with my conscious self?

In retrospect, I suppose I have been a bit disconnected. While trying to stay in tune with everyone else's needs, I often forget about my own.

I get caught up in the daily grind of my work routine, too often forgetting the tried-true rule of thumb that beginning my day with a focus on my spiritual nourishment will foster overall wellness in myself. The result will ultimately trickle out over my entire day and the people in it.

It is comforting to know when our bodies and minds veer off course and even when our intellect may be unaware - inwardly, we still have a spiritual compass, a divine navigation system in place. To send us little signals that we need to reconnect with ourselves. That we need to plug into our pasts to remind us of how much we have grown, that we need to focus on our present so that we may appreciate the gifts that surround us, and all this will nourish us as we move forward to all that the future has in store for us.

As my mind slips back into the past, my present becomes enriched, and I am comforted in the knowledge that the future holds the hope and promise of better days.

Because when we veer off course, our great navigator, with His silent directions, will always steer us back home.

The Community Building

I grew up (and still reside) in a subdivision where all the streets bear the name of a fruit, nut, or some other garden reference. When I think about it there is some irony present in that my heritage, my roots have borne much fruit on this land in this subdivision.

It began with my grandparents Frank and Rose, both immigrants. My grandpa (Frank), whom I was not blessed to have met as he passed either before I was born or right after, came over from Yugoslavia. My grandma Rose (who not only was I blessed to know but whose teachings I remember fondly), came over from Italy. Neither of their families approved of the union as they were marrying from outside of their heritage, something I can feel proud of today where tolerance and acceptance outside of constricts is celebrated. They were ahead of their time in their beliefs, and they were not afraid to risk it all for truth and love.

But I digress.

My parents also bought a house right down the street from my grandparents.

My parents met while my dad's older sister (we called her Dottie), lived across the street from my grandparents. It was no coincidence that God placed both families in a place where his plan would unfold.

Since then, my brother, myself, and two of my nephews have all planted roots right here in the subdivision whose streets all bear the names of fruits, nuts, and other garden references.

On one of the streets, Berry, I believe, there was a building in the center of the street that was referred to as, The Community Building.

The residents of our little subdivision, our little garden community of family and friends, could rent the space to hold gatherings. My extended family alone held numerous baby showers, bridal showers, weddings, etc. in this little building. Many, many wonderful memories were made in that place situated in the center of our subdivision, which at least for my family played a very central, important role.

A community building, to bring the community together. There were fish fries during the Lenten season and countless other activities held there.

Then they tore it down. After many years of neglect, the building was finally condemned. What happened to this little grand central station of activity? The people (my parent's generation), who volunteered for all the activities, the upkeep, held all the parties, passed on and the next generation (mine), well we just simply didn't take the initiative. We all had other things to occupy our time. Too busy, not interested, ya da, ya da, ya da. Combined with the fact that baby, bridal showers, and weddings these days have almost become a thing of the past.

Now that I'm older and it is my generation getting closer to the passing on phase, I felt sadness when I drove down Berry Street the other day and seen the empty lot which once served as the foundation of the little community building. So much has changed in this garden-named community, except the presence of my family. Our roots remain firmly planted and perhaps a new generation of volunteers will rise and build a community effort to bring people and families together, to carry on traditions, bear fruit, sow seeds of moral goodness, where countless future families will reap the many blessings planted within the community.

Strength, tolerance of our beautiful differences, core values that foster love and peace. I am proud to be a part of our garden community bearing the name of fruits on every one of its streets. Oh, and there are a few nuts too.

A Blast from MY Past

Yes, we are time traveling this week. Monday, I took you back to July 2021. Today let's skip a beat to this past April 2022.

Mickey Dolenz of the Monkees is doing a concert at our local theater - Rialto Square, and I - HAVE TO GO, are the words I had been telling my husband. And GO we did. Our seats were in the perfect spot for ME to travel back in time...

April 2022:

When The Monkees television show first aired, I believe, I was three years old. It aired from 1966 to 1968.

I hardly think that at three years old I was watching The Monkees on television, and probably not at five years old - when it ended. But never-the-less my earliest memories are of me on Saturday mornings lying tummy down on the sixties carpeted living room floor of my parents' home to watch The Monkees. Most likely it was reruns of The Monkees, playing on our console television set. All I know is that moment in time is one of the fondest memories I have of my early years, watching the show, and daydreaming about Davy Jones.

This week my husband and I went to the Mickey Dolenz concert at our local theater. He is on tour doing a tribute concert to The Monkees, and boy was it good.

When I first learned that he was coming to the Rialto Square Theater in Joliet I told my husband I must go. Not, I would like to go. Not, wouldn't it be nice to go? - No, I said I HAVE TO GO.

For me it was kind of a turning point in my life. The band I grew up watching and being in love with now with one band member left is going around the country performing. I just had to be there. It's like the end of an era. His and mine.

Now that is sad in many ways and at the concert, I shed tears during at least three to four songs. Why? Because I felt like I was viewing my life in fast forward motion. But wait, where was I when it (my life), was happening, I found myself wondering?

I found myself admitting that my life is closer to its final performance, and I have yet to perform. I have yet to do the things I am supposed to do during this life journey.

I fear (in the wise words of the late Wayne Dyer, or whomever he may have heard them from) that, I may die with my music still in me.

That frightens the hell out of me.

I can't!

I simply cannot die with my music still in me.

For if I do my whole life would have been for naught. And if I do the people in my life - those most near and dear would not have experienced the gifts that I was supposed to leave them with.

Leaving the concert left me with many thoughts, unanswered questions, an emptiness and - a spark. A newfound determination to find that little girl who lied on a sixties carpeted living room floor watching The Monkees TV show, falling in love, and dreaming of the person she would become.

She MUST become because it would be a shame if she were to die with her music still in her.

Thank you, Mickey Dolenz, for a trip down memory lane. A place I needed to travel back, to find the road that will ultimately lead me back to ME, and the person I was born to be.

It's time for this daydream believer, to make her dreams a reality.

The Squirrel's Almanac

There is a bit of wisdom that I follow, at least I think it is wisdom although I do not know where I first heard it. Perhaps from my mom, who was the heart of wisdom.

It goes something like this; If the squirrel nest is towards the end of the branches, it shall be a warmer, milder winter, if closer to the trunk it shall be a cold, harsher one.

So far it has been my experience- it is gospel.

It was just last fall that I went out to take some photos of the beautifully colored leaves, the last of which were still hanging on before they took their final leap to the ground for a long winters sleep.

What a gorgeous day it was and although I had been dragging with the virus, I simply had to venture out of the house to enjoy the warm pre-winter weather before it suddenly in a blink would decide to change.

It was then while I was out enjoying the tapestry of colors painting such a beautiful autumn day, that I noticed the squirrel nests on a couple of the trees whose leaves already chose to make that leap during the first round of breezes that came to usher in the beginning of a new season.

I then looked over at the enormous maple tree that was in the front yard of my childhood home right next door to my home (where my brother and his wife now live).

The tree was damaged during a summer storm and part of the tree (two huge branches) had to be removed for safety reasons.

I noticed looking up at the tree, bare of leaves, and branches that there was no squirrel nest. Not a one. It made me sad. It was a stark reminder to me that so many of the traditions and people (family) I love (who also lived here on this street), and who we celebrated traditions with, have passed on.

I immediately spoke out loud the words "I miss you guys", referring to my mom and dad. And just across the way from my house lived my grandma and my aunts and uncles. My mother also grew up on this street and some of her siblings remained at the childhood home throughout their lives. We lost the last of our aunts just a couple of years ago, my uncle (her husband) still resides there.

I have but one uncle left from my mother's side of the family. He lives further away so we seldom see him.

However, I noticed him over at my brother's one day last fall. They were all out in the back yard visiting. He was wearing a mask. No doubt because just across the fence there were COVID cases - me, and my family. I was unable to visit with them. I was only able to give a wave of my hand and a holler of how are you?

Since I wrote this last fall, moms enormous maple tree was taken completely down by the county. The damage from the storm had left it too dangerous to leave standing. Now there lies as huge and empty space in my mother's yard as her passing has left in our hearts.

There have been so many changes in my life and in the lives of those I love. I wonder if I will ever feel those old-fashioned homestead feelings of yesteryear. Although we still celebrate those same traditions within our household, for me it is just not the same. It leaves me with an empty feeling that has grown even larger since the virus, political nonsense, and worldwide unrest has disrupted so many lives.

But as with all heartache and setbacks there is only one thing to do.

Move on. Move past. Create beautiful, new memories while continuing to celebrate old traditions. Sure, they may feel a little different, but their importance remains the same. Their center will always be FAMILY. And they are exactly what will keep those memories of yesteryear alive.

So, I will continue to look for the squirrel nests in neighboring trees and maybe the squirrels will someday relocate in the sister tree (of that enormous one that once stood tall in my childhood home). From a seedling of that big maple, stands an exact replica in my front yard.

Our family legacy lives on here in this neighborhood. I can feel my loved ones in the breezes that pass through the leaves of trees. I can hardly wait to celebrate Thanksgiving and Christmas.

It's going to be another lovely holiday season. Different, but lovely just the same.

Autumnal Equinox

Already?!

As much as I love the season of Autumn I can't help exclaiming - ALREADY?

This week on September 22nd marked the Autumnal Equinox. First day of Fall! And Mother Nature is fully aware as she has quite fittingly brought in much cooler temps. It is feeling like fall here in the Midwest.

But wait, I was not quite through with summer yet.

So let me reminisce and take a step back to June 21st when the Summer Solstice took place. The first day of SUMMER! For me it has always been the beginning point for my favorite time of the year. SUMMER!

I am a moon child. I was born in July in the astrological sign of Cancer.

I have always enjoyed every season, with all the natural beauty and elements as well as the traditional, and holiday fun each season brings. But without a doubt, Summer has always been my *favorite* time of the year.

It is, after all the best possible season for a water sign such as me. The warmer temperatures feel most comforting to my skin, as often I can feel chilled. It's not unusual to see me wrapped in some fleece on a summer evening when the air dips into the lower 70's. For me 80- and 90-degree temps are welcomed.

But I think the main reason I love summertime so much has more to do with my family than my love of warm weather and my birthday.

Growing up, summertime signaled in a time for lots of family gatherings.

Family Picnics.

Fireworks on the Fourth of July.

Swimming.

Outdoor games played with our aunts, uncles, and cousins like *Mother May I, Red Light-Green-Light, and Simon Says.*

Just typing the names of those traditional games brings a warm sensation throughout my being and a welling up of tears in my eyes.

Oh, how I miss those days and more than that, the loved ones who celebrated with us.

Lining up our lawn chairs to watch the fireworks at an old family friend's homestead, now that house is gone. It was moved to make room for another strip mall.

Even if the house was still occupying the same spot, all the surrounding build-up, blocks the view to the stadium where fireworks had and are still shot up every July fourth. But no commercial progress, or blocks of buildings can ever *block* the view from my memory of all those wonderful Fourth of July gatherings. They will forever burn bright in my heart. Those memorable times were some of the best materials that built the strong family foundation I have been blessed to be a part of.

One of my uncles would always make sure there were plenty of sparklers for all the kiddos. My aunts would tell us stories of when they were young and share their special memories of growing up.

We are blessed to reside on the same street that I grew up on as did my mother, my aunts, and my uncles. Hearing old stories retold of days gone by when they were children growing up on this street, in this neighborhood has been a favorite not only for myself but for my children as well. Those times hold a prominent place in our memories and in our hearts. And the loved ones who shared them are dearly missed.

This last Fourth of July that we celebrated was one of the better ones in the last few years. It was celebrated with just our immediate family and a couple of our kid's dear friends. We swam, grilled out, and watched fireworks from our own backyard. We stayed up late and listened to music, old and new, and *new versions of the old*.

It was a welcomed escape from the usual grind of our everyday lives. A much-needed relief which was needed by all.

I hope the tradition continues with our family's next generations and they too enjoy the summer months and all the special moments it brings. I hope they have lots of childhood memories to share and that they will continue to share those of old with the younger generations.

Aside from the cooler weather it naturally brings, I also love the season of Fall. And a part of me is feeling quite inclined to have another backyard get together to usher in Autumn with pots of chili simmering and cozy backyard fire pits a blaze with warmth and glow.

The summer officially began on June 20th - the Summer Solstice.
And the summer officially transitioned into fall on September 22nd - the Autumnal Equinox.
Before long mother nature will surprise us one morning with snow, ice, and frigid cold as the season of winter unfolds.

For me, every season is welcomed. Because each holds special times and special memories from the past as well as new hopes, dreams, and a chance for new memories to be made in the present for future generations to hear retold.

It is not just the natural elements of each season - a welcomed change in climate, holidays, and traditions, it's the people you share your life with that make every day, every season, every aspect of life great.

Create Your Space to Embrace Your Place

It is said - home is where the heart is. I believe that to be true. But if your home doesn't mirror your heart, then it will always lack the necessary element that makes one feel - at home.

If you create *your space* to your liking, then you will be able to fully embrace your place, in life. You will be completely content, and comfortable in your surroundings.

You will not want for outside stimulation because your home will fully energize you. You will feel motivated to care for your home and its inhabitants. Menial chores will give your heart delight. You will not want for anything in return because your beautiful home and your happy existence will completely fill you.

There is no place like *home* that radiates with a presence that gives you a sense of belonging. There is no place like *home* that embraces you with a warmth that can never be fully captured by any other place on earth, that one might find themselves dwelling.

Home holds the memories that built us.

Every person's life is made up of both good, wonderful, happy memories and every person's life is made up of hurtful, unpleasant, sad memories. All of it is like an ever-rolling tumbleweed that just keeps bumping and rolling about on our life's path. Some pieces of the tumbleweed are kept intact, some pieces are meant to fall away. Some pieces hold on until eventually an obstacle comes along, that forces their grip to give way.

Fill your home with the things that bring you joy.

To some, a home filled with many different things hanging on walls, perched atop tables, dressers, and floating shelves is considered clutter. To others that clutter tells the story of their lives. It represents family vacations, special milestones, important people that came into, and fell out of their lives. It tells bittersweet memories of loved ones lost, lost souls found, hopes and dreams that came true, and some that have yet to bloom.

Every person's home is a depiction of his or her soul, the essence of their being.

Sometimes when we share our homes with others, our essence somehow gets lost in the shuffle of furnishings, knick-knacks, and things. The dominant personality of the pair takes over (usually unknowingly), and the home takes on a vibe true to only one half of the two. When this happens, it is inevitably sure to leave the other feeling a sense of imbalance.

They can spend years wondering why on earth do they not have a sense of joy when there is everything to be joyful for? They cannot understand their lack of contentedness and it brings about a state of depression, which for some, never get a strong enough hold to pull themselves out. They can never quite put their finger on what the problem is, what their unhappiness stems from. They only know the sense of always wanting something else. Never feeling comfortable. Always lacking motivation to do the menial chores that need to be done. They love their families, they love their homes, but there is always "something" missing. Something outside of their grasp. Something they long for but know not what it is.

It takes courage for a person to live their truth. To show their true feelings and vulnerabilities. To insist on and stand up for what they want, what they need, and to not allow anyone to stifle their essence from being and thriving.

A person's whole being must inhabit a house to make that house a *home*.

And for a home life to be in balance, its essence must be a combination of the two. And, when that home is filled with other members, children, aging parents, every soul must have their own place to grow.

Each person must have his or her own *space to embrace*.

Everyone needs to be able to create his or her space - *to embrace their place*.

The Maple Tree

I was looking out the window the other day and noticed the gigantic maple tree in the front yard of my childhood home. My mother passed in 2017. We built our home right next to her in 2002. My brother and his wife own the home now and reside there.

Last year brought some horrific storms (of course right), the year 2020 itself was a horrific storm. The tree was damaged considerably, and a large section was removed for safety reasons. The remaining tree was left and although it is still gigantic, the removal of the two very large branches that were damaged left the tree looking quite sparse.

It dawned on me while looking out at it that it now has a marked division.

That got me thinking of how ironic - that division is almost a representation of our entire society as of late, but even more so during the horrific storm (as it were) of 2020.

The divided tree signifies our divided nation. And although it too still stands, there has been a marked change in its appearance. To some that may seem an improvement, to others a detriment. I (like the tree), tend to be divided on issues and I like to lean a little in both directions. Nothing in this world, in this life, is black and white, and I think as humans we must be able to see the gray, all the gray areas that lie between the black and white.

Today the tree, is being completely cut down. Unbeknownst to my family the county had marked it to be removed after it was initially damaged in the last big storm. For safety reasons it is better to have it completely removed.

Perhaps for the good of all, the division of our nation should be removed as well.

After all a tree divided will eventually fall.

And so it is, with a nation.

Goodbye Big Gigantic Maple. You probably don't know this, but you held upon your big, gigantic branches some significant memories for myself, my family, and all our neighborhood friends. So, I thank you for the beauty your massive trunk and lush green leaves gave us to behold. I thank you for the numerous days of shade on many a hot summer day, before we got AC in our house.

Yes kids, I survived no AC in the summer.

I will miss you, tree. I will miss checking your branches in the late fall to see where the squirrels made their nest, to predict the severity, or mildness of the fast-approaching winter months.

It is a bittersweet day for me, seeing that big old maple cut down. My mother always feared it would fall on our rather tiny (compared to the tree) house. I am sure her Heavenly influence has something to do with making sure it is removed now, before it does fall on the house. I think of my mom and dad every day. Living right next door, keeps the memories alive and keeps the wound from losing them, stinging. But today is a reminder that none of our loved ones lost are ever very far away. They are near, looking over us, keeping us safe and making sure no gigantic trees fall upon us.

God Bless, be safe, be well, love your families, and take care of your trees.

The Bottom Line

A little observation and advice to "*Self*"...

I'm letting past regrets steel away happiness.

My present memories are being pushed aside.

I can't possibly get the most out of the *now*,

If the *past* is where I choose to waste precious time.

The moment I take my next breath,

Should be the only thought that occupies my mind.

Take my advice girl...

Enjoy the moment you're in.

That's the bottom line.

Nowadays

When I was young my mom would use terms (as do I now, as an adult), that I would guess, much of the young *nowadays* have never heard of, let alone understand the concept of, terms and phrases like...

Make Do

In a pinch

What not

Save for a rainy day

Sad because now more than ever the principles of those terms may become a necessity, for surviving our current reality.

Our nation is suffering. Hopefully this new year will produce a lessoning of that suffering.

People with the gift of knowing past ways will survive best during the new norm wave. But the younger that were not taught the wisdoms from years ago - how will they survive?

How will they - make do, in a pinch?

Will they save for a rainy day?

Will they keep close in their hearts those little what nots, that hold the wisdoms of the past.

And with all the changes that we've seen and the more that are most likely on the way - will they survive from what they have learned from nowadays?

Vacation of the Heart

My heart is taking this week off

To simply wade in its sorrow

Basking in the sunshine of the day

Not troubled by uncharted waves, of tomorrow

Loss and grief are not emotions to be swept under, you see

But rather to ride with

Drifting out into the vastness of lonely

Feeling every pang

Through every degree and stage

For it is only by engulfing yourself in this feeling of sorrow

Drenching yourself in tears that after loss, surely follow

Can you arrive back on steady, dry land

Able with hope and strength, to gain the emotional ground to firmly stand

Loss is hard

Change is scary

You ask how on earth will I get back out into the world of the living and of loving?

Allowing vulnerability to once again peek outside of my walls?

The answer is simple

Give it time

Take a vacation of the heart

A week off to simply wade in your sorrow

Keeping your head above the tears,

Basking in the sunshine of the day

Let your mind be saturated with memories,

Feeling with every tear you shed,

their everlasting embrace

Mom, Dad, and Supper

After celebrating Mother's Day just this past weekend, I naturally have been thinking a lot about my own mom and her life.

This July will mark my 56th birthday.

I find the time I spend driving around all day to be very therapeutic. I get a great deal of thinking done. While driving today the thought occurred to me, where my mom's life was when she was turning 56? After pondering that for a bit, the realization came to me that when my mom turned 56 it was within one year and ten days from the passing of my dad (her husband).

My dad passed on February 25, 1994. My mom turned 56 on February 15, 1993.

Unbeknownst to her, or anyone, within just one year and ten days from her birthday she was going to be a widow. It's disturbing to think that in such a short amount of time her life changed so profoundly. All our lives did but for a wife (or husband) to lose their mate, I can only imagine, must be an extremely difficult grief to suffer.

My Mom and Dad met when they were in their teens. In those days it was not uncommon to marry young. You married young, had your babies young, and for my parents at least, became grandparents young. You worked hard to raise a family and then when the last one left the nest, you retired and prepared to enjoy life.

For my parents it didn't quite work out that way. My dad had just barely retired and before he or anyone knew it, he was diagnosed with cancer and was gone within a couple of months.

From the time they met, they spent every day of their lives together. Neither had outside friendships or activities that took them away from each other, or the family. If they went out (which was rare), they went together. Vacations were a family affair.

My mother was fortunate to be a stay-at-home mom and wife so naturally our home was always kept like a fine-tuned machine. House was clean, there were always plenty of groceries (she shopped once per week on Thursdays). A nightly meal (we called supper) was always prepared, and we generally ate together at the dining room table.

I envy my mom, having been a *work outside of the home* mom and wife most of my adult life, my household runs more like a "beater". Groceries are bought much more sporadically, and fast food enters our front door on many a night, and with everyone doing their own thing, going their own way, with their own way too busy lives, dining together at the table is mostly just on holidays. As I write this... it saddens me.

Now today, while I reminisce about my mom on this *post Mother's Day* Wednesday, I wonder if she *had* known on her 56th birthday that she would have just one year and ten days left before she would lose the love of her life, what, if anything would she do differently? How would she choose to spend her time? What words would she make certain to say if she knew she had just one year, and ten short days left to say them?

If I could ask her, I'm sure she would have plenty to say about what she would do differently. We are of course our own worst critics. But if you're asking me, I can tell you that being the most devoted wife any man could ask for, she couldn't have done anything differently because everything she did was nearly perfect. And words? She only spoke with the kindest, not just to her husband but to every human being that she met.

For myself however, it's a whole different story. I lack *greatly* and have much room for improvement. And so just in case, when I turn 56 on my next birthday, if there is any chance that within one year and ten days, my life may change drastically in a way it did for my mom (God willing it won't), I think I'll start right now to make the most of every day, say ALL those words that I should say, keeping the ones I shouldn't - mute. I will put everyone I love, above all the things that don't matter. Because life is precious and way too short.

And if I had but one more day on this earth, I would happily spend it cleaning my house, buying the groceries, cooking a meal to serve and eat at our dining room table as a family...and I'd call it supper.

Circles

Of life
Of friends
The "inner" when you've managed to reach *more* than just your ends
I believe history repeats itself
There was a beginning
There is a middle
But there is no end
We travel our journey and when it's over
It all begins again
We see it in the weather
The seasons know it's true
Fashion trends will *forever* bring old styles back to new...

I for one love seeing fashion trends that I grew up with, on my own children. It brings a bit of nostalgia to the air.

The other day while standing in line at the Cinema I noticed the boy in front of me was wearing frayed, slightly short pants (we used to call them "flood pants" or "floods") and sneakers. It was a pleasant sight, and it sent my mind immediately back in time. Which for the most part was a nice place to be, *to visit mind you*, I wouldn't necessarily want to go back.

It all reminds me of the old saying - history repeats itself. Ironically the more history I have under my belt (so to speak), the more this old saying seems to have a ring of truth to it.

Humans just seem to go back and forth with many things, not just fashion. We don't like something, so we come up with something new. Make all kinds of claims that the former was bad, and this one is much better for you...at least until we get bored and come up with another - *new*. And round and round we go.

Yes, the past is a nice place to visit. And some fashions (in my opinion) will never go out of style. But I think I'll stick to enjoying the NOW while looking *forward* to some wonderful "news" in the future.

Drive-Thru Homes

Do Our Lifestyles Rob us of Our Peace?

What once were dwelling places, now are merely pit stops. Empty places we stop to shower and sleep. Most of the time, not even staying long enough to cook a meal and eat.

Our jobs and our activities have become our entire existence. They are the things that surround our day. The *events* of our lives have become the *homes* where we stay.

It is this mobile way of life that is robbing us of – *our life*.

Most of us do not have lives we just have a series of events we do day after day.

Ask someone what they did today – the answer will be a list of taxi driving kids around to various activities while running errands in between.

I would be willing to bet that none will answer – "I went for a walk."

"I enjoyed a nice lunch."

"I picked one flower that led to a bunch."

For humans to survive we must RECLAIM our lives!

How can we run our lives if we continue to let our schedules run us – ragged?

With every seemingly important event that *we run to, we are running away,* from our lives. Our *dwelling* must take place in our *homes* and our *hearts*. We must put our vehicles in "park" and stop living our lives - from our cars.

Sanity cannot survive.

Life will not thrive -
if our engines remain in "drive"

9
AUTUMN

Ahh...FALL

Nature's nourishment for the soul

Tromping through the dew-wet green
With each step of my feet
The slightest hint of crunch
Whispers underneath

FALL is upon us
Time to nestle
Time to sit
Time to ponder
What makes my heart tick?

I have begun a new routine.
With two days in, I'm hoping it sticks
Ah well, I guess that's all up to me

I walk to my cabin before my day starts
To commune for a bit with my beating heart
Visit awhile with my soul

Asking the questions, by this age, I should know
What does make my heart tick?
What gives my step its light kick
with just two days into my new routine
I know for certain
it is this

TIME
Spent with ME
It's the medicine these old bones need
Tromping through the dew-wet green
With each step of my feet
The slightest hint of crunch
Whispers underneath

A short little walk with the morning air breeze
Out to my cabin where peace does exist
And I can experience it with even the shortest of sit
If only a bit
Stirs me
Nature's nourishment for the soul
Serves me
What I need

Tromping through the dew-wet green
With each step of my lightened feet
The slightest hint of crunch
whispers underneath
Ah...FALL

Withering Life

Even a gloomy sky can be beautiful, *nonetheless*
when the backdrop for an autumn day
Accompanied by a slight breeze
Leaves tumbling off their trees

Under the sun
limbs grow their buds
There they cling
surviving the rains of spring
on branches, they call home all summer long
With one burst of autumn air
They are gone

A beautifully colorful sight
red, orange, brown
cover the ground
Green Earth carpeted
with a vast array of bright
seemingly overnight
For the eye of the artist, a visual delight

Our lives imitate nature
as seasons change
So do we
People, places, and things fall away
Leaving us with that gloomy feeling of bare
Certain parts of our lives we grew accustomed to
Suddenly, no longer there

As we prepare our hearts for the cold days ahead
When winter makes the earth her sparkly white bed
We take stock of all that was
Keeping bits and pieces tucked in our memories
to visit now and then when we are feeling down

We look at the ways our lives have grown
From tiny buds hanging on for dear life
Once a burst of seasoned breeze blows
We are suddenly as frail
As the withered leaves that tumble from trees

Our winter season begins
Our time to rest is now
And although it appears gloomy
Nonetheless, it's beautiful
Somehow

Energy – working WITH it

Tune into and connect with your energy, especially during late Fall when the world around us begins to draw on it the most.

The holiday season is pushed upon us early by the world - we can halt our absorption by conserving our energy with meditation, rest, and creating calm in our homes and practices.

Take each holiday in by enjoying it in full. Do the rituals from childhood - bring each alive with fun, relaxing, nourishing activities.

The world can be full of the hustle and bustle of the season, but we can stay nestled in our safe zones by nurturing and celebrating ourselves.

Gift a gift of peace to self. Staying plugged into your inner needs - will keep your energy levels at optimal speed.

Meditations for Fall

Gratitude and Abundance

Thanksgiving is upon us, and it is customary and expected that time is set aside from one's busy festivities to take stock in and give thanks for our abundance. To count our blessings and to be grateful. We give thanks for our lives, families, communities, and all we have that sustains us - food, clothing, warmth, water, electricity - the list is unending. Also unending is the number of those among us that do not have plenty.

Many are in need, some quite desperately. We must halt our busy lives and even busier minds to listen. Often listening requires us to have eyes to see. By not taking blind eyes to the injustices that surround we are open to behold those in need. Our hearts give from what we have, to share.

Sometimes the person in need is us. Many of us are in desperate need of physical and mental rest. Some of us may need a reprieve from the emotional merry-go-round that life sometimes traps us on. We cannot possibly help a world in need if we are needy.

So, during this week of Thanksgiving - let's take a breather and practice gratitude not only on a world level but also on a more intimate level with ourselves.

Be grateful for the inner voice that whispers desires to your heart.
Your inner voice prompts, reminds, and warns.
Listen to it.
It listens to you.
It hears your stirrings and knows what blooms joy into your being.
It protects you from an ego that likes to insert fear and doubt -
those are the times' inner voice resorts to a shout,
in the form of an aching, nagging in your mind when
"something" doesn't seem to sit just right -
listen in your quiet space.
And once you have replenished the needs of *your* soul -
go out and do your share to make the *world* more whole.

Meditations for Fall

Rest and Release

Be present in your life NOW.

Give yourself the rest you require.

Reward yourself with rest.

Accept who you are NOW.

Give gratitude to the steps that have brought you to this space.

Release the unnecessary burdens that upon yourself, you've placed.

Welcome and embrace your YOU.

Give yourself an inner hug.

Everyone needs a hug every day.

Each day we come into our lives whole, but *life* has a way of *breaking* little bits of us throughout our daily lives. Giving yourself an inner hug is like soldering those loose pieces *of you* that the world has been picking - back in place. So, with a warm, alive flow of love for self - HUG - securing *your wholeness* back in its authentic space.

Happy First Day of Fall

Growing up in the Midwest Climate Change was called Seasons.

Happy First Day of Fall.

Let's welcome in the change of season and with gratitude embrace a new climate, not only in our weather but also in our hearts.

August

Although the ending of my favorite season (summer), is not something I relish, I must say I do love the feeling that the onset of August brings.

The nudging that fall is soon to be upon us makes me look forward to decorating, wearing fall colors, the eminent approaching holiday season and all the joy it brings... it all begins, at least for me with the onset of August.

August means the fast-approaching start of a new school year and for me it means, (or used to when the kiddos were young), school supplies shopping. And although, I'll admit it was a little stressful at that time, what with a lack of money and cranky kids (and mom), now I have to say, I miss it.

In fact, I woke up the other morning with the notion to go school supplies shopping just for myself. New pens, a better stapler, some cool notebooks - why not? The approaching academic season can still be fun - for me.

In recent weeks I've been rearranging things, decluttering, and cleaning out, an organized home, *and life* being my goal. I really want to utilize my time better so that I can do more of the things I love to do - write, create art, READ an entire book!

So, I went on the lookout for a calendar organizer that would stimulate my desire to stay organized and not squash it by being too daunting. I mean let's face it, some organizers are just so complicated with all the stickers and various pages to ultimately fill in with the same info - it only creates more mind clutter for me and office clutter because I end up not using it so there it sits on my already too messy desk.

Well, what I found is an amazing alternative. Just a simple rectangular sized organizer with limited info dump areas. It's basic! It's perfect!

I can hardly wait to use it (it just arrived yesterday), and it has sparked in me the urge to go buy new pens, pencils, and hey maybe some cool markers to work on some of my doodle art projects...it's already working to get me pumped up for a new season and a desire to do the things I love.

Yes, the inevitable farewell, so long to summer is fast approaching and although I really hate to see it go, I am excited to usher in the Autumn Season with a big HELLO AUGUST - thanks for waking up my long-lost *mojo*.

Henny Penny

If you are not of a certain age, you probably will not get the reference to my title, but lately, I feel just like Henny Penny when she ran around the barnyard yelling, the sky is falling, the sky is falling.

Henny Penny, also known as Chicken Little, is a story about a chicken that gets hit in the head with a squirrel nut that falls from a tree and immediately assumes that the sky is falling and begins scampering all around the barnyard, spreading the news.

Akin to Chicken Little, I find myself completely falling apart over even the smallest of life's lumps that seemingly out of nowhere clobbers me.

I feel as if not the sky, but a big dark cloud is hovering right overhead, waiting for the perfect time to deluge me.

Whether it *the weather*, with its increasing hints that the snow, sleet, and bitter cold is just around the corner waiting to make my arthritic bones ache a little more, for a lot longer. The worry and suffering of the family loved ones over medical situations. Or the normal disfunction that berates our family as it would any family forced to cohabit well after the college years end.

Or perhaps, and this sounds more fitting, it is the slow-moving storm clouds that are covering our world with the fear of mass destruction if we all do not get our shit together and FAST.

I am not exactly sure of the cause but, I have just been out of sorts of late.

I have no reason to complain. Even living in a world with so many uncertainties, life here on our street, in our home, with our family and pets, is pretty darn good. And I am so grateful for the many blessings we have.

Still, there is this constant pricking at my psyche that says there is something brewing. Some things are just not right. That at some point, people who have been keeping a lid on it are going to blow their tops.

Now here within my walls, we are cool. We do not necessarily let the chaos surrounding us permeate our fortress.

But the toxic fumes smoldering in the cities, states, countries, the whole damn world around us are beginning to pollute our breathing room a little. Thus, creating a kind of fog within my usual chipper self, and as I said, I feel like chicken little running around saying the sky is falling, the sky is falling -

Because the world in which I grew up is most certainly falling apart.

Keep Yourself in Line

With only good vibes.

Set your intentions for the day.

Wake up your senses.

Breathe in the cool clean air.

Start your day without the slightest of cares.

Set intentions you can ride.

Like a wave effortlessly gliding across the oceans tide.

Ride the wave of your day

with only good vibes.

Keep yourself in line.

11.11

Today is November 11th. That's 11.11. Which means Make a Wish. Which means your thoughts are being manifested as you think them. Which means - KEEP THEM POSITIVE. THINK POSITIVE THOUGHTS. MANIFEST THE REALITY YOU WANT IN YOUR LIFE, IN YOUR WORLD.

Today is also Veteran's Day. So, THANK YOU, THANK YOU, THANK YOU to all the real heroes. Those who have served and are serving to ensure our freedoms are and will always be a reality.

Now back to that positive thinking. I say let's all commit to do some TODAY on 11.11! And let's bring even more magic to the moment by doing it at 11:11am and 11:11pm.

Here are some suggestions on what we could as a unified energy manifest...

Health, wellbeing, love, honesty, integrity, wholesomeness, oneness, unity, generosity, prosperity, goodness, more love, forgiveness, compromise, compassion, fearlessness, sharing, stability, awareness, and the list can go on and on.

Just one rule.

KEEP IT POSITIVE :)

10
ENDINGS

The Souls We Could Not Know

I know that I will not know you

Until my time on earth fulfilled

Had I known

I would have moved

Heaven and Earth

That you be allowed

God's gift of birth

I would have knelt

and begged our Lord

Please do not allow

These young hearts

be hardened now

Please strike fear out of the way

Let hope shine its message of brighter days

Let Your peace fill the hearts

of these two

who now choose

I would have prayed had I known

That their choice be life

But I know, not His reasons

And can only trust they are

For some higher purpose

this tragedy was allowed

I do not question His why

I only ask for His guidance now

In our grief to show us how

And not just for them and me,

for this will affect many more than us three

So, until my time on earth fulfilled

I will love you from afar

You will be my precious darling

No matter where you dwell

Though my heart remains broken

And my eyes with tears swell

I know someday I will hold you

Kiss you on your cheek

Cuddle and rock you

And bounce you on my knee

You are my darling angel

Who will remain forever in my heart

Even though I did not get the chance to know you

I will see you in every blooming flower,

every butterfly that flies,

and in every star shining bright in the darkened sky

I do not blame your parents

As I know, they also are sad

And are wishing somehow now

time

could be turned back

And another chance to choose

had

A different choice I know they would make

Their tears show how much their hearts now break

Again, we cannot answer why

Things happen

And we do not understand

How can a tragedy

Also, have God's hand

Be in His plan

But faith tells me although He most certainly does not ordain

He lets the choice be ours, just the same

And He will open our hearts and eyes

And we will realize

the how

the why

In the lessons, we will learn

Until then, I will hum you a lullaby

As I lay down to sleep

The dampness from the tears on my pillow

As in it, my sadness seeps

Please know that you were, wanted

It was fear that ripped you away

With the uncertainty of the situation

And the effect on the everyday

I know that she did not mean for things to happen quite this way

I know because she is mine

And I have no doubt

if it were in her power now

She would turn back the hands of time

God's love allows for forgiveness for every living soul

And the promise we will someday be united

to the souls, we could not know

In the days ahead, I will strive to accept

And keep you in my prayers

Until my time on earth fulfilled

And I return to Heaven

Where I will hold you then

I am still your grandma

And between the veil, my soul sees

Until the Lord calls me home

Heavens beautiful angels

are holding you for me

rip, baby

Hoping Twenty-Twenty-Three Will Be Better Than the Last Three

A while back, during one of my many *start overs*, I went to the gym to do some cardio. Previously when I had been there, I was motivated by the fact that although a slight raise in my heart rate made me feel as though I would surely drop dead off the elliptical machine - I did not, and I felt great afterward, which was the fuel that propelled me to get my __ __ __ there that day.

Unlike the previous, I felt less like I was going to die and more like I was going to feel great afterward - a good sign, I would say.

While working on cardio, listening to music via earbuds - televisions lined up in front of me, though mute to my ears. Looking at the array of programs airing, I realized I had a choice of what I wanted to fill my head with and to which TV I would give my attention. Which program would influence my mind? That choice was mine. There were sporting shows, antique picker shows, shows I was unsure what they were about, and then amongst all those were the news media shows broadcasting the only event that was huge at that time on the news.

The horrific war on Ukrainian soil. The unimaginable horror that the people in Ukraine were facing. Are still to date.

It occurred to me that they did not wake up the day hell became their reality, with a choice of what they were to watch or listen to while they enjoyed the freedom to work out at the local gym. No, they would only hear bombs exploding in the not-so-distant areas where planes were dropping them. Unable to insert earbuds to bop along to the tune they wanted to listen to, what rang in their ears was gunfire from soldiers invading their promised land - for reasons that were only important to one. One whose authority was causing others to embark and fight for reasons they did not agree with or even understand.

While the rest of the world went about their ordinary existence, an existence that at any given moment could also be disrupted by bombs and gunfire and radical evildoers that think they have a right to dictate lives.

Are we a human race? Or are we barbaric robots acting without moral consequence? If we do not believe in what a deranged authority commands us to do, are we to do it anyway? No!

We must ALL do right by everyone on the planet by saying NO to those who want to destroy simply because of their insane, outrageous thoughts of what they believe the world should be.

The Ukrainian people said NO!

What are the rest of the people of the world saying? Give them an inch, and they will take a mile. Give a country they will take another, and another, and another, and another, and when they do, are we ready to fight? Will there be anyone left to fight?

That day I was at the gym listening to music play in my ears. Thankfully in a free country. Free is not as the word is defined. Free came at a cost to many who said NO and were willing to fight.

I never want to get my work out on a battlefield listening to bombs overhead and gunfire before me.

No one does.

No one does.

There are no winners in war.

But when peace prevails,

Everyone does.

We have a great many wars going on right here in our own country. The freedom that we have taken for granted IS at stake. Depending on which news show you watch, you may or may not believe it. But the bombs nor the people dropping them won't wait to have believers. They won't wait for you to make a choice. We will have no choice but to fight, to say NO.

As a free country, we can instead fight at the ballot box. I suggest we equip ourselves with the armor of truth, before we head out into the combat zone of political flyers. Do your homework. Vote YOUR conscience, not a political party's agenda, nor a media's spin.

I'm hoping the **Party of *Humanity*** Wins.

Jumping Off vs Joining the Band Wagon

Next time you commence to beat yourself up about falling off the wagon, and filling your head with fiction about your worth, ponder this little story...

*The wagon went full on all the way to the edge of the cliff and off it and **they** all went.*
*Those who fell off the wagon before it plummeted the edge of the earth - remained **grounded** and safe.*

Moral of the story, it's the trials that strengthen us. It's those circumstances that shake us to the core that ground our roots deeper to weather future storms. In our most sorrowful moments, a glimmer of hope waits for joy to abound.

Don't follow the band's wagon, follow your own. Be YOUR true self, not *what or who* others attest to, or think of you.

So next time you fall off your wagon, just rise, stand strong on the safety of your solid ground...and ride on.

Message Received

If you were to receive a message from a family member, friend, anyone special in your life, or maybe just from a neighbor or acquaintance you may have crossed paths with at some point.

If that person were to say, today I know is my last day.

Would you like to pay a visit?

So, we might say goodbye.

Chat a bit of what it's been like,

Having you being a part of my life.

No doubt your answer would be, YES of course.

I'll drop what I'm doing now, to spend this last bit of time with you.

And you would be quite touched no doubt, that in their last few hours they thought enough of you to want to spend some time, when minutes to them - are few.

That is the scenario of which nothing is true.

For we just never know when our minutes are nearing - few.

We will never receive such a message, so embrace every second now.

Whomever you may cross while on your path, leave a positive vibe behind.

When you speak, say something kind. Instead of glaring with a frown, share a thoughtful smile. Remember karma pays back; the choice is yours if good or bad.

Life is short we all know.

Yet we all find excuses to ignore.

Don't wait for an invitation.

Don't wait for a knock at your door.

Decide today,

Concerning those you love, invest more.

The only commodity that really matters is time.

Everyone has it.

Everyone wants more of it.

Everyone spends it frivolously,

Thinking there will always be enough left to enjoy.

But when it is gone,

It cannot be earned back.

It's forever lost.

If a Hurricane is Coming, RUN!

Or better yet just breathe.

When a storm of negativity comes flying at you like a hurricane

And harsh words come a whirling, your heart the aim

Make a decision to get out of the rain

Don't let the emotional flood of others, slip you up

Nor allow the force of their destruction pull you into their *negativity* rut

Instead, inhale a long breath from deep within your gut

Then exhale, *for your karma*, their wrath away

Don't allow the shrapnel of someone's wrath tear *your*, self-worth apart

Arm yourself with virtues, wear them as a spiritual hood

Surround your entire being with the energies of *good*

Joy, peace, serenity - food for the soul

Keep your vibrations at a level that rise you above

While other's storms may ensue

You always have *your* choice to lead by example, be just, be true

Do whatever it takes to elude

Passing on your goodness to everyone you journey by

Breathe in, breathe out carry your step light

Keep your emotions grounded

And rise

Bite Size Life

When we take on more than we can chew

In life

We gulp

Through the moments of our days

We cannot savor the time that passes

Leading to missed opportunities

Lost moments to cherish

And a life of churning heartaches

We must digest

Loss

I can't even imagine the pain one feels after losing a spouse. Recently a close family member is having to experience this. In a vulnerable moment he conveyed a small glimpse of what he was *and is* feeling, and it touched me. It made me wonder what that could possibly be like, to be in his place right now. And thus - I wrote this fictional portrayal of what a day in his life right now, might feel like.

Side note: Please cherish those you love, for we just don't realize how one moment can truly be the last.

Beautiful fresh cut flowers, adorn a pearl white vase perfectly situated on an antique entryway tabletop. The colorful array of blooms mirrors those that also adorn the garden just outside the quaint, charming side porch of this house with a country flair.

The vase, in and of itself, is a testament of beauty with golden embellishments winding around the pearly hew of its body. Its breathtaking beauty is a hint of its class and elegance. A family heirloom, passed down from generations but never finding its truest beauty until placed in the hands of - my wife.

The house is empty and as I enter and close the door behind me, I am consumed by the deafening silence. I glance at the vase, which looks exactly as it did when I left the house less than a week ago. The blooms appear fresh despite the air of death that now lingers.

I glance towards the staircase across from the entrance and my eyes are drawn upwards to the landing atop the stairs and to the rail just outside of our bedroom at the top of the stairs. My mind wanders to memories. I am consumed with memories. How can a simple staircase, how can looking up at a landing spark so many memories fusing through my exhausted mind?

I realize it's because I am not looking at just a staircase, or just a landing. I am reliving a staircase lined with holly berry garland and sparkling lights and grandchildren making their way down those stairs with anticipation and excitement on their faces - wondering what Santa left under Grandpa and Grandma's Christmas tree.

My eyes well as I gather strength. I set my hat on the sofa in the living room where I left her, less than a week ago. She was sick and I was headed to the hospital for surgery. A surgery I was not able to postpone any longer although I wanted to. I wanted to stay in that living room. I wanted to tend to my sick wife, my wife who, a month ago was cleaning up after her family, my wife, who cared for everyone with the attentiveness of a saint. So much so that she often ignored her own health concerns, her own personal needs.

I sit on the sofa and look towards the spot where year after year, she put on display for all our enjoyment, the most spectacular Christmas tree one could imagine. More magical than Santa could have done himself, every ornament hung artfully and with so much love and devotion to her family and our traditions.

How can a week's worth of days hold the weight of a lifetime of sorrow? How can you wake one morning to joy and fullness and then wake to another day drowning in the deepest part of lonely you have ever experienced?

As I ponder this, with the heaviest heart that I could ever have thought would hang in my chest, I get up, walk past the staircase and enter the dining room - her dining room. She made that room the most special room of the house just with her elegant presence adorning it. Many hours she spent doing what she loved, singing. Her voice filled the room on the many days I walked past, back and forth going from the kitchen to the living room, out onto the porch just outside the den. Back and forth past the staircase, up the stairs, outside, downstairs, to and from work. Did I hear her then, when her voice was painting the walls of that room? Did I notice the smile on her face when she sat there with her grandkids and played? Did I appreciate the many meals she cooked, the holidays she hosted, the weddings and funerals she attended with me? Did I see her standing beside me during the most trying times of my life? Did I tell her enough *I love you* and *I am so happy you are my wife?*

She brought the beauty out in that vase by the entryway door. She made the staircase come alive with excited pitter-patter of children's toes, past the holly berry garland with tiny pinecones. She fostered traditions making magic unfold. She cared for her family, protecting like the feminine lioness she was. And she touched the hearts of so many with her friendship. There has not been a more devoted daughter, sister, mother, and wife.

My wife, YES, I did hear. I did see. I did appreciate and I will forever miss my love.

There has been loss. I have suffered the pain of losing many, many loved ones. But the empty I feel now is nothing I have ever known. The depths of this empty, is not contained by the description of words. There is no way to describe. How does one begin to tell the story of oneself, separating from one's life source? When you have lost your lifelong mate, you have lost the largest part of your own being. Your very own existence is threatened. How can half a heart, beat? How can half a soul feel joy, how can only memories fill my being with the energy needed to survive –

after losing my wife?

I sit in the dining room, and in the deafening silence I hear not with my ears but only within my heart - my half a heart, the whisper of the Lord - you can do all things in Christ who strengthens...

Faith fills my half a heart with enough energy to carry on and I trust, will continue to sustain me until the time comes for me to once again be joined to my wife. When my heart will become whole again and my soul will be fully filled with joy.

Until then I will spend many hours walking through that entryway, admiring the lovely staircase, enjoying holiday decorating with family in the living room and sitting in this dining room where the essence of her soul remains. In the silence I can hear her precious voice bouncing off the walls. And though I am empty with loss, this house is forever filled with her song. RIP - SKZ

Endings Lead to Beginnings

I think it is safe to say the ending of 2021, much like that of 2020 does not hold the same bittersweet nostalgia that other passing years held.

I would bet that every person on the planet is gleefully bidding *good riddance to* yet another year of pandemic hell.

Unlike nearly every other aspect of our existence, this is surely a time when we *are* united in our thoughts, our opinions, our hearts, and our desires.

But, though highly anticipated and welcomed, it is still an end. And endings typically are sad. Endings mean loss. Endings mean having to let go when we are still grasping at straws to hang on.

Endings are saying goodbye before the hello has left our lips.

This is true, especially of the last two pandemic years we have faced. Many loved ones were not even permitted to say goodbyes. Even as heartbreaking as it has been for those who lost their lives, those that had to carry on enduring the pain of not being able to spend last precious moments, even if those moments were to say - goodbye.

But endings are the only paths that lead to beginnings. And beginnings are where we find hope.

Joy abounds in beginnings. Newness, wonder and delight are all found when we embark on something new, something different and unknown. Beginnings are what raises our pulses, quickens our heartbeats in anticipation of what is to come.

Beginnings can also hold our emotions hostage in fear. But the greatest joy comes from conquering those fears, owning our emotions, rising to the occasion and overcoming. Holding ourselves accountable and NOT letting fear, nor our emotions rule us. The sense of accomplishment we get when we step out into the unknown, and DO IT afraid, stays with us and fuels us into the next battle with our fears.

All this happens during the endings and beginnings we encounter while on our life journey.

The difference is *ends* are often covered with shades of sadness. While beginnings are saturated with bright hues, bold and colored with hope.

Goodbye to the drabness of 2021!

Hello 2022!

I think it will be colored with much brighter days and bringing with it hope for our world.

Happy New Year.

Six Days

September 29th, seven years ago, seems like yesterday

My phone rang

I struggled to comprehend as I listened in disbelief

to the voice on the other end, consumed with grief

Holding back my tears

I offered to come and console

I turned the car around when a whisper told me NO

Though your love for them is like family, the reality is - you are not

Let them console their own

If needed, they will let you know

Heading back, I made a stop

My phone rang once more

just as I was entering the store

Another call

That struck time still

My mind was already in a fog

From the previous phone call

I answer to hear my mom crying for help

Her voice trembled with the sound of tears shed

I assumed for the baby and her unfathomable death

I wondered "how could she possibly already know?"

Then I realized it was not for the baby that she cried

But for reasons of her own

I flew

through crowded streets of cars

My gut ached with grief, and terror consumed my thoughts.

What was this horror?

What was this nightmarish dream?

What the hell just happened?

And what was about to unfold

that would leave our hearts with an un-mendable hole.

I sped across the driveway

Over the grassy green

The ambulance she called was already on the scene.

Entering my childhood home

My mom, in typical character, reached out to console me.

It will be ok, she said between the coughs

Later, in intensive care

I held back my tears to keep a positive vibe in the air

while a tube kept her voice silent, she managed to mouth

It's ok.

While she lay still, she was listening as my guts spilled out all over the room.

As a daughter, I had not been the best

And how I wished I had spent more time being a better friend

I apologized for being less than I had thought she'd hoped.

My tears soaked her bedside.

She heard as I whispered to my own aching heart my hopes for resolutions to heartaches long past

And I held her hand for six days straight until she breathed her last

And then I held it longer, praying my love could bring her back

But it didn't

And she was gone

September 29th was an ordinary day

Six days later

ordinary life changed

lost was a lovely baby who lit up our Skye with bright

We lost our beautiful mom who gave our world its beaming light

All the necessary tasks that required tending to in times as these

Were carried out by her loved ones, navigating with blinders of grief

The last goodbyes said

Before leaving the room, Detective Me spotted something just beside her bed.

It was a small round eraser like those found on a mechanical pencil head

and the imprint on it read

The word - OK

I picked it up

I couldn't believe my eyes

I tucked it in my pocket, safe and sound

She continues to comfort

With Unspoken words

Never far from our hearts

Just beneath the veil
she comforts from afar.

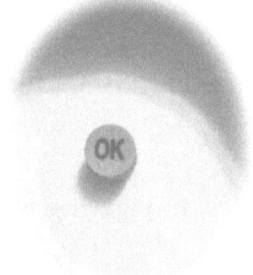

Fly Free Butterfly

I live in a smaller community in the subdivision that I grew up in and many of my relatives also still reside. There is a certain camaraderie, a certain unspoken alliance between the neighbors of our neighborhood that we have each other's back. We feel each other's pain when difficulties or tragedies strike. Even amongst those that like to complain and nit-pick, over barking dogs, burning leaves, or parking in non-allocated spaces, when push comes to shove, they too are there to lend a hand and show support of their fellow neighbors.

Yesterday I heard terrible news of the sudden passing of a neighbor on my own street. He lived in the house my best friends grew up in, and I spent a great deal of my childhood in.

I don't have many details except that it was sudden and of course a great shock to the people of our little street where everyone has each other's back and of course to his loved ones as well, I'm sure.

My thoughts are with one of the young neighbors that spent a lot of time there visiting, sitting out in the evening looking up at stars while having campfires in the same yard that I spent many an evening doing the same, when I was her age. I wonder how I would have felt if one of my friend's parents would have suddenly just - been gone. With no understanding of why, just suddenly- not there one day. And how, as a youngster I probably would not have had the skills to be able to process the obvious feelings - fears that would have undoubtedly come to surface. How I, as a shy introvert would have kept all that bottled up to try to swallow on my own.

And now I wonder, what would I say if I had the painstaking task, how would I as an adult, explain to that young, innocent heart why it is breaking so with someone she cared for suddenly being - *just gone*, today and forever?

I would say, to this young precious soul, that we as humans on this planet, in these bodies are kind of like caterpillars, when in the cocoon.

We are trapped here in these bodies, on this planet unable to fully be the free spirits that we truly are. And when we pass from this cocoon (of life), we can fly free like the butterfly, magnificent in beauty and grace. And, although the caterpillar changes from caterpillar to butterfly - the creature is still present here on this planet, just in a different state of being.

Now instead of crawling about the earth, toiling through existence, to be trapped in the cocoon of life, our neighbor is now flying free like the butterfly, full of beauty, of grace, *and* still with us - just in a different way.

Yes, that's exactly what I would say to the innocent heart that grieves today - when suddenly - in an instant someone she loved is - just gone.

I would say to her, no, he is not gone, just free....

Just like the butterfly fluttering beside that tree.

RIP Neighbor.

Road Blocks

Tragedy doesn't come with a calling card.

Alerting you to its nearing.

It just shows up,

And you find yourself in the wake, of its clearing.

Frightening times in the world around us, can toss us into an unsettled mode.

But we must keep our faith strong, and our resolve on that which we know.

One God, *our God* is ultimately in control.

And He will bring about good,

From hardships, that block our lives roads.

Tragedy doesn't call before it comes.

Sometimes - it just implodes.

Rage

The new virus is rage. It has swept through our nation, our families, our hearts. It has torn complete cities and livelihoods apart. What is the cure for this new strain of disease? Speaking for myself, I'm going to begin the research - with ME.

In the last few weeks my life has been catapulted with Rage. In my own family there has been angst, anger, hurt, and sadness. All the ingredients that form the perfect soil for rage to grow. And grow it did.

And then we have the world outside of my bubble.

The unrest in our society, whether you believe it is all part of an orchestrated plan with a sinister intent or a spontaneous act stemming from injustices faced by many whose emotions have been on an ever-increasing low boil for generations.

Either way you choose to believe, the result is the same - RAGE

Sitting from the inside looking out it is easy to see clearly all the ingredients being added in this recipe for disaster, one at a time, to bring about the outrage. But when rage finds itself boiling up and over within *yourself* it can take you and others by surprise.

My point is that we are all capable of RAGE.

It can affect all of us - if we let it. And I did. I did in the name of fairness. I wanted to see first-hand what all the RAGE was about. But doing so only brought the disease into my own heart. And I lashed out with rage filled words to describe how my heart was affected by some of the poisonous ingredients that were used which tainted parts of our system of justice. But the aftereffect of this new virus becomes worse than the beginning symptoms of it and I found that what happens is the very thing you are enraged about - you become.

There is no difference

RAGE is RAGE.

And it is never justified. An eye for an eye is not the message we were taught. Yes, thinking and feeling that way makes you feel justified when you are amid injustice, but in the end, it is the condition your heart is left in that will define true justice.

As humans we can only do our best to be as honorable as we can be, given our many inherent faults and weaknesses. So, we need to put on a layer of protection every day that will shelter us from the ingredients that can make our hearts vulnerable to the disease that has gone viral - RAGE.

This, in my opinion is the only remedy that will bring about the cure.

It can wear different masks; this disease and it often disguises itself in what appears to some as righteousness. But make no mistake, it is infectious, and it aims to kill the very souls it claims it acts to protect.

The Real Virus - ultimately is fear.

I'll say it again. The real virus - is fear

FEAR is what has gone viral in this Nation and the entire world.

Everyone is afraid of what they cannot control, of being on the bottom of a presumed pyramid of superiority and successfulness. But we are all on the same playing field. We are all on the same level. Because we are ALL human. ALL of one *(no matter the name you choose)* Creator. WE ALL MATTER from our conception to our death and beyond - every human life MATTERS. And unless we want to become extinct by our own doing - we had better start treating each other as if we all matter, BECAUSE WE DO.

Let us all be an ointment to each other. Let us all protect each other from any further spread of this disease of fear by eliminating at least one of the worst and destructive of its symptoms - RAGE.

Back By Popular Demand

Death is a natural part of life, of living.

I know this and usually can mentally and emotionally prepare myself for the inevitable when I am faced with the reality of death due to a loved one's battle with illness. However sometimes the universe decides to throw one right out of left field and it knocks you completely out of your normal, evenly balanced mental state – into a whole new emotional ballgame.

You lose someone just out of the blue. Didn't even see it coming. Even if it was in the case of someone ill, all was going seemingly well, right? They were doing fine. Their condition stable, for what you thought would be awhile. Suddenly their number is drawn, and time stops, for them and for you.

It has been this way for me for the last couple of years now. Beginning with the loss of a sweet baby girl, my own Mom, my aunt (*and Godmother*), and now just a couple of days ago, a dear, treasured, most precious friend.

All these losses along with a few other heartbreaks in between have left me – kind of empty. It's caused me to kind of ignore myself, my health and my household is suffering. Their deaths have left me - dying.

Well, it must stop. Life does go on and I must go on with it. I have decided to reclaim my *quality* of life. I must do the things that I love doing to keep me in love with living. Writing is one of those things.

My daily Author Blog is another one of the things that has also suffered. What began with a daily writing time has slipped further and further from my routine. From daily, to weekly, now is at best, maybe once a month!

Recently some of my readers expressed to me a sort of loss that they had been experiencing - MY BLOG. Wow! I didn't realize there were people that really enjoyed *daily* my thoughts and written expressions. How happy this made me and boy has it motivated me. I am very humbled by this sharing of love and enthusiasm for something I love to do, and it has ignited that spark of enthusiasm that I had when I first began it.

Now of course my busy life no doubt will infiltrate my time, and my blogging time may get shifted in the shuffle here and there, but it will take its rightful place back in my daily routine, just as rising and breathing does, because it makes me feel alive. And with so many losses that I have taken in this game of life. ALIVE is a really great place to be every day.

Happy Monday.
Whether sweet or sour - Enjoy every morsel of it!

Lines

We cross them every day.

For some it is the end of the…

For others a starting point that is sometimes difficult to put that first step forward.

You can draw them in the sand. At Disney you can stand in them for hours on end.

Often, we meet people that refuse to see them when they infiltrate our space.

The older we get we accumulate more of them on our face.

They are all around us.

In music and in art.

When a child colors outside them, we tell him he's a star.

Grownups like to keep safely inside. Abandoning their colors for a life of black and white.

Reading in between them can broaden your view.

While focusing too narrowly causes minds to shrink too.

A story can have many and still not be very good.

But a poem can be a masterpiece by having just a few.

Lately there have been straight lines on machines that blink and buzz.

Accompanied by a long unannounced and deafening hum.

The beginning of the end for so many that I love.

Now the only lines I see are those that make a long-wet streak, across my cheek from the many tears I cry.

Another soul was added to the "cancer victim" long line.

I wish we could have had *one more* for old times' sake.

Before he stepped across to where the hands of Jesus waved.

He had a good run though not long enough.

There's never enough time.

And far too many lines.

RIP Dana ~ you'll always be precious to me :(

Everything Else Will Follow

I have been steered away from my course of late. It's easy to do. Getting off track. You might even say it is inevitable. Distractions are all around us and staying focused on the goals we set can be a challenge.

Persistence, consistency, accountability. All elements to successfully staying on track with your goals. For me and the goals I have made for myself, a few other elements come to mind.

Be armed and ready before you begin to ensure you reach the finish line.

Now, as usual, I tend to overdo (with everything), so of course, I don't have only one goal. That would be too easy to meet. No, I have several. But one that is on the top of my list is with my health and getting back in good shape. Thankfully I already have good health (aside from a little cold bug). But in good shape? No. In fact, I can't remember the last time I had a real work out. Ten minutes of stretching and yoga here and there doesn't count. Nor does the fact that I am always *on the go*. Being busy and constantly on the run when your form of movement is an automobile puts me under the sedentary lifestyle category. I hate admitting it, but it is the truth.

So, will I make it to the finish line with this goal? Only time will tell but having my armory well stocked will certainly make it more a possibility than not. *The first step*, eliminate the goodies. I don't mean move them to a cabinet I don't often go in. That's what I usually do rather than pitch them, *with the mindset that someone else may want them*, and so why waste? No more. I hereby give myself permission to WASTE and PITCH. If someone else wants a goodie that's their problem. I'm not making it mine anymore. *The second step*, fill those cabinets, the ones I frequent *and the ones I don't* with healthy foods. And fill the refrigerator too. Then *keep* it stocked. Make the time to get to the grocery store so that I'm not stopping at the fast-food shop. *Thirdly*, GET MOVING. Out of the car and into the gym, the park for a walk, in a spare room with weights, whatever it takes.

I feel good about being successful with this and all the goals I have set of late, and the reason is that I am finally remembering to do what works. Taking care of myself is always the best way to start. And when distractions come around, and they will it's never too late for everything to fall into place.

Just begin and everything else will follow.

Sugar Junkie, back on the wagon again

Serendipity - Coincidence - Happenstance

Or whatever you like to call it. You know, those God Instances' (as I like to refer) when the universe lets you know that everything is working like clockwork. I find it absolutely amazing and find myself (mouth dropped open) in awe, every time it does. Today I was blessed with it happening on several occasions.

Not only does the universe let us know when all is going as planned, but it also shines a bright light in our eyes when we need to see things more clearly. From my prompt today, the question posed to ask ourselves was "What am I addicted to?" My answer was **"what am I NOT addicted to?"** Now, most people think that if they are not dealing with a drug, alcohol, gambling, or sex addiction problem, then they are not addicted to anything. I say, WRONG. In fact, I would surmise to say that every single person on the planet is addicted to something. Think about how much time we spend on our devices (phones, computers, media in general). How many workaholics are out there? For me it's coffee, the white stuff, (that's SUGAR, HA, got ya), staying up too late, and overextending myself with projects. it seems nearly everything I do, I OVERDO. Lately, though my biggie has been sugar and overeating in general, and it shows. Not just on my frame but in my mood. You can't feel good when you know full well that you are not living good. Everything is connected, mind, body, spirit, and when any part of that dynamic is off, it throws everything out of whack.

Today nearly everything I tuned into was speaking to me about sugar and how bad it is for us. I know this, yet I keep allowing myself to let it take hold of me, just like an addiction *does*.

It never fails to amaze me how the universe stays so connected to an individual's path, sending you the messages and wake up calls at precisely the moment you need them.

The good news is, tomorrow is a new day and although I will begin it with one of my addictions, *coffee* (which I will happily remain enslaved to), I will be drinking it black. :)

What Part of NO Don't I Understand

what part of NO don't **I** understand?

So here I am on day three of the new year. Due to my lingering winter cold, I have not stayed on the *morning* ritual I had envisioned for my - *striving for a more centered, wellness-focused life* - plan. But kudos to me for sticking to the *ritual* at least, though later in the day, sometimes right at bedtime, still I am doing it. Today's "prompt for thought and reflection" in the Daily Stoic Journal (my bible for the new year) talks about saying NO. Saying NO to those people and things that monopolize your time and leave you, drained.

So, my first NO is going to be spent on ME, my hair appointment to be exact. This is a rough one for me, though being sick makes it much easier (obviously I'm not going to go while sick). But it's more than that, and yesterday I said NO to make-up! Again, made easier due to not feeling well but on the bigger note what I am saying NO to is those non-necessary things that rob me of time and money.

I so look forward to my hair appointments and by the time one rolls around, my mood desperately needs one. There is something about graying hair that puts a damper on the psyche. But my saying no is not just due to being sick, I could possibly be better by Saturday. My pocketbook, however, will not. So, saying no means living within my means. I am determined this year to rid myself of these little things that add up so quickly, in years and in dollar signs. Does this mean I am never again going to color my hair or wear make-up? I hardly think so. Both of those things do add a lift to my mood, but if I have to say NO occasionally until I have the extra cash, that's exactly what I will do. Doing so will aid me in my quest for peace. And who knows, I just might feel good while graying. It could be a very freeing experience. I may just decide to keep it. Why not embrace my true self? It's all about feeling content, and being at peace with myself, my choices, and my surroundings.

So, it will take practice learning to say NO to those who tend to drain me of my time, money, and resources, BUT the most challenging will be saying NO to myself, and the even harder part will be to obey (ME).

11
WINTER

Release Your Artist

Pain sews a thread of poetry.

It's woven deep within the fabric of the hurt.

Pulling, ripping at the very seams that bind you

You wonder where you might find relief.

When will there be an end to the grief?

The only way to expel it

Is through your art

Let it pour, *pour* out of every scar that has formed around your soul

Release your Artist.

Let your rage spew an array of colors on the canvas.

Let your ache paint a poetic picture of your broken heart

On the pages from the scrapbook, you've just torn apart.

Let your inner voice sing its song of blues

Let the musician climb out of you.

The greatest artists known

Wrapped their broken hearts

With the fabric from the hurt their pain had sewn

And all that is left are the remnants of the art

That depicts the healing of a soul.

Clearing Out Space

Making space is something we should get in the *habit* of doing.

Clearing out space in our homes, and *figuratively speaking*, in our minds, bodies, AND habits, is imperative for our overall well-being.

Just think of how we allow habits to clutter our time. Clear out your *time space* and see how much lighter you feel. Enjoy the emptiness this creates in your place and your *inner* space.

Clutter in the home lessens your ability to move freely and comfortably.
Mind clutter stifles you from being your authentic self and living your authentic life.
Unhealthy eating habits clutter your body with excess weight causing a lack in energy to experience the life meant to live.

Making space in these areas frees up more room to be who and what we were born to be.

Making space is one habit to keep!

Embrace Change

Change is essential for growth.

It's evident in the nature surrounding us (our natural environment) and our natural selves.

Throughout our lives, we endure changes in our bodies, minds, families, our circumstances - everything needs to grow. Everything needs to *change* to do so.

Welcome and embrace it. Look forward with excitement and anticipation. Like a gift - change is *present* in our lives for a reason - in *every* season. At times personal change feels harsh, and we often feel unprepared. When we encounter this make time to take a meditative walk reminding ourselves with each step - nature navigates change with ease, and so can we.

Whatever season of life you are in, whatever the climate surrounding you brings, rest in the knowledge that through change, we grow into the beautiful blooms, we were created to be.

So, give yourself a well-deserved EMBRACE *for a change*.

The Sky is Not Falling

Although my mind and heart are in full Fall mode, the sky - has decided it is wintering time.

It's just a week before Thanksgiving, and the weather has turned to winter virtually overnight, at least here in Chicagoland. Last week it was in the seventies. This week, well - it's cold enough to snow AND STICK!

But back to me and my mindset - we are still Falling, at least for a bit longer. And here are some of the ways I am doing just that. Feel free to join in.

Meditations for Fall *(from page 263, again relevant)*

Rest and Release

Be present in your life NOW.

Give yourself the rest you require.

Reward yourself with rest.

Accept who you are NOW.

Give gratitude to the steps that have brought you to this space.

Release the unnecessary burdens that upon yourself, you've placed.

Welcome and embrace your YOU.

Give yourself an inner hug.

Everyone needs a hug every day.

Each day we come into our lives whole, but *life* has a way of *breaking* little bits of us throughout our daily lives. Giving yourself an inner hug is like soldering those loose pieces *of you* that the world has been picking - back in place. So, with a warm, alive flow of love for self - HUG - securing *your wholeness* back in its authentic space.

Quiet is a Beautiful Sound

In stillness much energy is found

Not doing allows one to accomplish more

Opening a heart to its inner core

For in all of this

awareness becomes most clear

A soul becomes more closely in touch

with the things we see and hear

And to our purpose, our steps draw near

Spend time today in silence

Let it surround

Because quiet is a most beautiful and the most productive sound

Sad

I feel an eternal sense of sadness throughout my core.

I can only speculate it is because people are sad, all around me. And I am sad, completely. I am sad because they are sad, because I have *caused* sadness, and because they have caused *my sadness* equally.

The whole world has a cloud of sadness that has been building for many millennia. During different eras the storm cloud of sadness bursts and we have tragedy, worldwide uprisings that force us to take shelter in our grief. Retreat until we can regain a sense of calm, stability, sunshine in our lives that can radiate out into the world until once again there is joy, happiness, tranquility, even if only in disguise.

We all carry with us a piece of this universal cloud. Periodically it covers us and rains upon us. And when the gush of its deluge subsides, we again reclaim a sense of balance in our lives.

For the last couple of years, I have chosen a word as my *mascot word* of the year. It always carries with it a goal for a better me, a gateway to get to where I want to eventually be.

I am leaning this year towards the word RESILIENCE because I think we will always have sad clouds peeking out of our sunny days within the realm of our individual lives as well as worldwide.

But with resilience we can ride the waves. We can see through our rapidly whisking windshields of frenzy that a smoother road ahead is just beyond the downpour. With resilience we will get there. With resilience we will arrive back at happy every single time.

To fool yourself to think there will ever be a day of no sadness, no storm clouds, is dangerously walking a tightrope, the outcome being your fall from fantasy straight into the pit of depression, deception, and despair. We cannot fool ourselves into thinking that those bad things don't exist. We can't pretend that in our lives there is only sunshine. Just because you look out from rose-colored glasses, doesn't mean the rest of the world doesn't notice the plummeting hail that surrounds you.

They do and it only makes you the fool.

We must embrace *all* the clouds to fully appreciate the sunshine. And when we are openly accepting of all the bad along with the good - it is there we can be a force of resilience in our world.

The Meaning of Life

Many people for numerous years have pondered just that — What is the meaning of life?

With regards to my own existence, I think I have finally pinpointed the main (one) thing. *And for those of you familiar with the movie (City Slickers) I am holding up my index finger.*

The meaning of life is to just simply LIVE it.

Just BE in it every day, the daily pattern, the ups, the downs, the good, the bad, and all the in-betweens.

Live all of it

Enjoy all of it or hate all of it. No two days are the same. But all the days put together — that is where the meaning lies.

We spend so much time (at least I do) trying to figure out how to do it better. We lose precious time of it.

We complicate life so much with the meaningless, that we skim over the meaningful.

Like starting a book that doesn't keep our attention quickly enough, we flip through to the end to see how it ends and to decide if it is worth finishing. We are not willing to thoughtfully go through each chapter, each page, giving it the time and substance it so richly deserves. We think if it is not great all the way through, why bother.

We take no joy in living through the story. We get in a hurry to jump on to the next, and the next and the next. Trying to find the right thing that will hold our interest. But that is all wrong. With life you get what you get and if it's not great all the time, make it better.

Lest you get to the end, and you feel your time was wasted.

When you get to the end, your last page is filled with questions.

Why didn't I?

How could I have?

WHAT was the meaning of my life?

Why the hurry? Why do we want to go through so quickly during the early years? Once the end comes it is after all the end, our end.

Now as a Christian I happen to believe there is life after. But I also believe that our after life will be that much sweeter if we take the time to truly learn, grow, and enjoy our earthly life first.

So, for me the meaning of life has evolved to one very simple truth.

LIVE life and life will have meaning, day after day, page after page, year after year, chapter after chapter and when you arrive at The End - It would have been time well spent, learning your life's meaning, while living your life's purpose, and enjoying the whole story as it slowly unfolded.

Be Your Own Valentine

When doing special, lovely things for our Valentines this year...

Let's not forget to take care of our own hearts this Valentines Day.
Let's be kind to ourselves.

For some this may be a habit already soldered into place. But for others (*present company included*), this idea may be foreign. However, this is the year for putting in place GOOD HABITS as well as replacing the bad. I am pretty sure I am not alone in this so let me make a few suggestions for us all.

For starters depending on your preference, sleep in, or if you'd rather, get up extra early to enjoy the quiet. Meditate, contemplate, or just simply enjoy a hot cup of coffee without interruption or noise.

Take care of your body, mind, and spirit.

Bless your body with a good stretch. Maybe do some yoga, take a brisk walk.

All day long, in between doing nice things for our lovelies, let's fill our minds with good thoughts, and silently chant positive affirmations to our inner selves.

And let's not forget to do a little something extra special for ourselves today. Take a long hot bath. Enjoy a healthy meal. Steal away some quiet with a nice cup of tea. Anything at all - just do a *something nice for ME*.

By the end of the day, I think you will agree in between the candy hearts, the assortment of chocolate in a box, all the little presents given and the thoughtful ones received...

It was a Happy Valentines for all, even for little ole ME.

Happy Valentines Day - Enjoy!

What is Love?

Baby don't hurt me, don't hurt me no more...
As the lyrics suggest. Love Hurts (another familiar song). Well, it's true. Love does or can hurt sometimes. But it doesn't have to be a fatal wound.

Even when love doesn't work out the way we thought it would, the pain and suffering we inflict on others, or allow them to inflict on us, doesn't ever *have* to happen. Yes, there will be pain and suffering simply because feelings are hurt, tender emotions have been rubbed the wrong way, there is disappointment, and what we thought we wanted, doesn't come to be. Notice I said, *what we thought we wanted*. I believe everything happens for a reason. Usually when we look back on any circumstance, we can see the blessing behind the blues.

But if we go into a relationship with the understanding and open mindedness that both people are individuals and sometimes life just happens. Sometimes things are not meant to last forever. Sometimes people come in and out of our lives for a purpose, for a lesson (either ours or theirs), and *only* for that reason. And no matter what, we all deserve to be treated with dignity and respect. There is no reason for hurting someone, with words or actions. If it is time to go, if it is time for a relationship to end - simply go, simply end it, allowing for both to move along on their own path without all the bad feelings weighing them down and without dragging along a bunch of unnecessary baggage (theirs or ours).

Let's not forget loving and being loved is a privilege. Being trusted with the vulnerability of another's heart is an honor and should never be taken lightly or for granted. And we should allow ourselves to be vulnerable enough to make our partner feel safe with the sharing of their vulnerabilities with us. And we should handle every feeling entrusted to us, with the utmost of care.

Just as importantly, we should use these same principals if and/or when it is time to go, when it is time for the relationship to end.

Be kind, be loving, take the high road ALWAYS, and continue your journey. The blessing will be obvious someday when you look back.

and you might even find yourself singing...
At last, my love has come along. My lonely days are over, and life is like a song...~Etta James

Glorious Day

Thank you, Lord, for this day and for Your presence here with me now. Thank you for taking my hand and walking with me through the up times as well as the down.

When I need to walk away from my comfortable space, but from fear I will not budge. You place Your hands on my shoulders to give me a gentle nudge.

When my heart yearns to see what's outside of my box, but anxiety keeps me locked in, you give me courage to explore the possibility of loosening my fearful grip.

You draw me back with guidance when at times I choose to leap, and by trying to walk too fast I trip over my own two feet.

When my eyes shed tears of frustration, you give me strength to bear.
When blinders askew my view, You patiently remove, with care.
When sadness lays heavy on my heart, flooding it with a rain of despair,
You give me a warm embrace to let me know You are still there.

When winds of rage swirl thoughts of uncertainty into my head, and my mood becomes laden with worry and dread, with the wisdom of Your word my starving spirit is fed.

When lonely fills my night, I find comfort in the twinkling stars above.
When the morning sky brings clouds that cover the sun, I feel Your smile upon my face, as you wrap me in the sunshine of your love.

And through the fields and roadways and the many paths I'll take, beside me I will feel Your hand holding mine along the way.
So I thank you Lord for *this*, another glorious day.

Wake Up!

My dream, as I could best recall -
Christmas
Some of those around me
Rather than offering me help to cope
Instead were glad to see my spirit had finally, broke
I awoke feeling exhausted
Like I had experienced this in real time
It made me stop and ponder
The effects of my racing mind -

A few months back I had a dream. The next morning, I vividly remembered the above highlights. At the time I tried to figure out what the dream might have meant. I jotted down a few lines fully expecting it would soon pop out of my head, like dreams often do.

I concluded that the dream was my inner self, reminding, or possibly warning me to slow down both in body and mind. It was Christmas time and as usual *I* was making it the busiest time of the year. And no doubt I was worrying about stuff, like I also usually do.

I find it fascinating how our dreams speak to us. I believe dreams are like God's telegraph, directly relaying messages to us about the things we often fail to see. Warning us about the inevitable pain and discomfort we will most certainly feel by the lifestyles we adopt.

Over-extending myself comes as natural to me as breathing. It's just something I do without even thinking about it. But just as my dream tried to remind me, over extending can and will be detrimental to my health.

So, before the hustle and bustle of the fast-approaching season arrives I think I will take some time to relax my body, empty my racing mind, and just breathe. And maybe I'll throw in an occasional nap and enjoy a good *dream*.

Play Your Cards

No Matter the Hand Your Dealt

Lately, I have been battling this winter bug. It's going around. It has gone through our entire house wreaking havoc in the body of every occupant, ending with me. Illness has a way of beating you down emotionally in an almost worse way than physically. You begin to feel hopeless that you will never feel better. I keep telling myself "As soon as I feel better (physically), I can get to the task of putting this place back in order from the whole holiday whirl." In my mind, I have the desire to get busy, but my tired-out body just isn't feeling the enthusiasm. I'm left longing to *get back to normal.*

Then it occurred to me, what if the way I am feeling (physically) right now, were to become my normal? What if I suddenly found myself with an illness that was going to linger and never leave my body at all?

Would I get on with the task of living? Or would I allow it to beat me the rest of the way down? Would I *fight like a girl*, or would I run like a coward?

We never know what obstacles life is going to throw in our way. But no matter because it is still *our* way. This life is ours to live as *we* choose. To take our scrapes and carry on, though bruised. We *are* strong enough to do that, if we choose.

Whatever it is that has become our new normal doesn't have to cause our happy to end. Joy is most often found in the simplest forms, and it can be ours if we choose. We just must be willing *when needed*, to bend.

We can still enjoy the rays of the sun, warm our tear-stained face. We can choose to be strong when we're NOT feeling brave.

So, what will I do if being sick were to become my norm? Will I let it make me stronger, or will I let my spirit break? Will I take the cards I'm dealt, or shuffle up a whole new game, raise the stakes, and continue to play?

Other Titles by this Author

A Cup of Inspiration To Go Please – *My Heart Runneth Over*
Heart Strings – *Forever Wanderer*
Locks of Love – *A Book of Encouragement*
A Line in the Sand – *A Journey Towards Forgiveness*

About the Author

Holly Coop resides in the Midwest with her husband, children, and furry friends.

Holly enjoys writing and publishing inspirational poetry, motivational quotes, and spiritual insights. She has authored five poetry collections. Touching hearts with words has become her life purpose. She hopes her words will stir hearts and inspire others in their purpose. In addition to writing, Holly enjoys sketching, photography, and creating art featuring her poetry.

HollyCoopBooks.com

A Little Backstory

In 2019 I decided to publish an Author Blog. A place to escape where my thoughts could run free. A platform to connect with other readers and writers and just enjoy the craft. Writing is like breathing for me. It is essential for my life. It sort-of evolved into a diary for me. Unlike my poetry blog where I primarily just posted poetry, this blog was more about things that were on my mind, and my heart. Various moments of trials, as well as celebrations. It has become a blessing to my everyday life, and I feel that I have grown in my craft since I began it.

I live in a community where of late several of our neighbors have become owners of chickens and roosters. The chickens are basically quiet, but the roosters are well - LOUD. Personally, they do not bother me, but I do see all the sarcastic comments on the neighborhood Facebook page from those with differing feelings on the neighborhood feathered friends and their daily dose of chattering (squawking?) — not sure of the proper term but you get the gist of it.

Nearly every morning while I'm sipping my morning coffee, penning my blog posts, I hear an orchestra of rooster calls in the distance. I recently had the notion to take my blog and transform it into my next book. I have accumulated quite an array of pieces and wanted something tangible of it that I could leave to my kids along with my other titles. I mean you never know, someday my blog might just be – gone with one wrong click of a mouse or stroke of a key.

One day while on one of my morning's walks, I was deep in thought and planning on how I would tackle this next endeavor. Well, my thoughts were interrupted by guess what? Yep, rooster calls.

Thus, was born the title *and* cover idea for this my sixth publication. I hope you've enjoyed it. Thank you for your support.

Blessings,

Holly

I hope the little nuggets of wisdom, whimsy, and woe...
will be carried with you
...while journeying through *forks* in the road.

The End

Post Titles in this book	Page Number
Opening the Door to NEW	Page 1
In Closing	Page 2
My Word for the New Year	Page 5
If You First Don't Succeed	Page 6
Seize Your Day, Your Way	Page 7
Cracks	Page 8
New Year Revolution	Page 10
Blue Swayed, Shoes	Page 13
Boxed	Page 14
It's Monday	Page 15
Notions, Yearning, And Choices	Page 17
Wellness Priorities	Page 19
Moon Wink	Page 20
One Word	Page 22
And the Universe Says	Page 24
History Repeats Itself	Page 25
Serenity – This Way, Serenity Found	Page 26
So Far So Good	Page 27
Hanging on by a Thread is Still Hanging On	
Tying Up Loose Ends	Page 29
Turn the Key	
Crucify	Page 32
Spring	Page 34
Today is the First Day of Spring	Page 36
And All That Jazz	Page 38
Have a Beautiful Day	Page 39
Is it Not Enough that I Bled?	Page 40
Earth Day	Page 41
Its Just Routine	Page 46
Tree of Life	Page 48
Happy Easter Monday	Page 49

Put Your Joy On	Page 51
Chicago Style	Page 54
Karma Happy	Page 55
A Character Flaw or a Spirit, Broken?	Page 56
How Brilliant is Your Life	Page 58
Let's Focus on the Human	Page 61
Negative Thoughts	Page 62
Don't Just Be a Spectator, Get IN the Game	Page 63
Lead Your Heart	Page 64
When Push Comes to Shove	Page 65
Crossing Lines	Page 67
The Energy is Within YOU – Release It!	Page 68
Wednesdays	Page 69
Grading Scale	Page 70
Dreadful	Page 71
Be Golden	Page 72
Kindness	Page 73
Good Vibrations	Page 74
Kinder-Garden	Page 75
Be the Bulldozer Not the Ground	Page 77
Gratitude	Page 79
EPA of the Mind	Page 80
To Be or Not to Be, the person I claim to be	Page 81
I Saw You Today	Page 82
Warning – I'm Gonna Use the F-Word	Page 84
Thoughts at Sunrise	Page 86
Dragonflies, Deer, and a Hummingbird	Page 88
Body Armor	Page 92
He Wants You to Know	Page 94
Tip Your Hat to A Woman	Page 96
My Shadow	Page 99
Spectacular	Page 103

Be Comfortable in Your Cabin	Page 105
Mismatched	Page 106
Behold	Page 108
Best Friend	Page 110
Yin, Yang, And Everything In-Between	Page 112
Let Go Your Ego	Page 114
Snack Break	Page 115
Practice Trolley Riding	Page 117
Normalcy	Page 119
Breakfast Groove	Page 120
Do You See What I See?	Page 121
Transitions	Page 123
Rethink Your Groove	Page 125
Limitless	Page 126
A Fork in The Road	Page 127
Stop Living a Rerun	Page 129
Breathe	Page 130
Calm Indifference	Page 131
What's Your Point?	Page 133
Plans? Don't Plan on Them	Page 135
From One's Extreme to Another's	Page 137
Out of Focus?	Page 138
The In-Between	Page 139
Shift Your Gears	Page 141
A Day with a View	Page 142
Mind Your Own	Page 143
Rock Steady	Page 145
Steady as She Goes	Page 147
Morning Treasures	Page 149
Music, Smiles, and Generous Hearts	Page 151
Singing Bowls for Healing Souls	Page 153
The Smell of Rain	Page 155
Myself, Coffee, and a Cat	Page 157

Here's to Birthdays – Past, Present, and Future	Page 159
The Music in Your Life	Page 162
Vacation	Page 163
Worship and Praise	Page 164
Birthdays	Page 166
Why This Lord?	Page 167
Discipline	Page 170
The Gift of Me	Page 172
Blame	Page 173
Stuff It	Page 174
Take the Extra Mile	Page 175
Breaking Down Walls	Page 176
H.E. Double Toothpicks!!!	Page 178
Mean Spirited	Page 180
Habitual Progress	Page 181
Be Happy or Die Trying	Page 182
Who is Holding Your Joystick?	Page 184
Back to Routine	Page 188
Bird's Eye View	Page 192
Revisions	Page 194
The Silent Treatment	Page 196
The Remedy	Page 197
Mind-Set – Reset	Page 199
Don't Rain on My Parade	Page 200
If it Works, Keep Working It!	Page 202
Self-Sabotage	Page 204
You – Control = Trust	Page 206
Is What You See Merely How YOU Perceive?	Page 208
Hometown Joliet	Page 210
Home	Page 219
Cosmic Connections	Page 223
The Community Building	Page 225
A Blast from MY Past	Page 228

The Squirrel's Almanac	Page 231
Autumnal Equinox	Page 234
Create Your Space to Embrace Your Place	Page 238
The Maple Tree	Page 241
The Bottom-Line	Page 244
Nowadays	Page 245
Vacation of the Heart	Page 247
Mom, Dad, and Supper	Page 249
Circles	Page 252
Drive-Thru Homes	Page 254
Ahh…FALL	Page 256
Withering Life	Page 258
Energy – Working WITH it	Page 260
Gratitude and Abundance	Page 261
Meditations for Fall	Page 263
Happy First Day of Fall	Page 264
August	Page 265
Henny Penny	Page 267
Keep Yourself in Line	Page 269
11.11	Page 270
The Souls We Could Not Know	Page 271
Hoping Twenty-Twenty-Three Will Be Better Than the Last Three	Page 277
Jumping Off Vs Joining the Band Wagon	Page 280
Message Received	Page 281
If A Hurricane Is Coming, RUN!	Page 283
Bite Size Life	Page 285
Loss	Page 286
Ending Lead to Beginnings	Page 290
Six Days	Page 292
Fly Free Butterfly	Page 297
Road Blocks	Page 299
Rage	Page 300

Back By Popular Demand	Page 303
Lines	Page 305
Everything Else Will Follow	Page 307
Sugar Junkie, Back on The Wagon Again	Page 309
What Part of NO Don't I Understand	Page 311
Release Your Artist	Page 313
Clearing Out Space	Page 315
Embrace Change	Page 316
The Sly Is Not Falling	Page 317
Quiet is a Beautiful Sound	Page 319
Sad	Page 320
The Meaning of Life	Page 322
Be Your Own Valentine	Page 324
What is Love?	Page 326
Glorious Day	Page 328
Wake Up!	Page 330
Play Your Cards	Page 332

345

www.ingramcontent.com/pod-product-compliance
Lightning Source LLC
Chambersburg PA
CBHW030450100526
44580CB00002B/64